CREATION
IN
SCRIPTURE

A SURVEY OF ALL THE EVIDENCE

Herold Weiss

Energion Publications
P. O. Box 841
Gonzalez, FL 32560

www.energionpubs.com

2012

Cover Design: Henry Neufeld
Cover Image: © Jorisvo | Dreamstime.com

ISBN10: 1-893729-48-6
ISBN13: 978-1-893729-48-3
Library of Congress Control Number: TBD

ADVANCE PRAISE FOR
CREATION IN SCRIPTURE

In this brief and concise volume, Dr. Weiss demonstrates the importance of exploring the entirety of Biblical evidence on this all too often divisive topic. With clarity and concrete example, he makes clear that this subject does not lend itself to simplistic answers. This volume makes a significant contribution to conversations regarding creation and the Bible. It is my hope that people of faith will use this helpful book to further future dialogue among those who value both Scripture and the human reason with which we have been graced by our loving Creator God! For those who believe that one can be both scholarly and faithful, this is a 'must read' book!

Rev. Dr. Robert R. LaRochelle
Author, *Crossing the Street* and *Part Time Pastor, Full Time Church*
Pastor, United Church of Christ

Most studies of creation in the Bible have focused on the first two chapters of Genesis, with little reference to the rest of Scripture where much discussion of creation is found. With characteristically wide understanding of the languages, and the historical and cultural contexts in which the Bible was written, and with deep theological insight and spiritual sensitivity, Dr. Weiss has made an important contribution toward rectifying this imbalance. Reading this book will reward everyone concerned with issues regarding the doctrine of creation.

Earle Hilgert
Professor of New Testament Emeritus
McCormick Theological Seminary, Chicago.

This is a "must read" book for anyone interested in the current discussions on the concept of creation in the Bible, its cultural context, and its relation to current views in science and evolution. It is authoritative, cogent, masterfully articulated. I've read widely on this topic and have never read anything its equal. It pulls no punches. Better yet, it is timely, wise, and faith affirming.

Lawrence T. Geraty, Ph.D.
President Emeritus, La Sierra University

Wading into the often truculent conflicts over creationism and evolution, Herold Weiss offers up the refreshing input of a biblical scholar who is fully attentive to the cultural contexts and religious variety of biblical traditions. While insisting that the life of faith and scientific inquiry each be given their proper respect, Weiss challenges those who would speak theologically about creation to consider more broadly the entire range of biblical evidence, rather than privileging a few chapters from Genesis. Crafted with great clarity and a wealth of knowledge, readers are treated to a lavish feast of biblical views of creation, from the prophets and Wisdom literature to the letters of Paul and the apocalyptic world of Revelation. What a remarkable little book: at once a bold challenge to creationism, exposing its reactionary impulses and indicting its ideological abuses of the Bible; and, at the same time, a generous invitation for thoughtful Christians to celebrate the amazingly rich and varied portraits of creation, and thereby to bolster their faith in the Creator in a way that is both well-conceived and biblically based.

Terence J. Martin, Ph.D.
Professor of Religious Studies
St. Mary's College, Notre Dame, Indiana

In *Creation in Scripture* Herold Weiss presents the essential message that the creation story is complex and is addressed in many ways throughout scripture. As it is, much of the hot debate occurs when people take one particular part of scripture, sometimes out of context and sometimes misinterpreted and then baptize this passage as the one and only infallible description of how God really created or creates. This is the first book I have seen that takes this "overview" approach and considers all the Bible's commentary on Creation. Kudos to Weiss for this contribution.

Richard Colling, Ph.D.
Author of *Random Designer*

This Book is Dedicated

to

my grandchildren

Jacqueline, Andrés, Elena

Daniel and María

TABLE OF CONTENTS

PREFACE

All Christians agree that the human world is God's by creation and redemption. For centuries Christians debated among themselves how exactly redemption has been, is or will be accomplished. The "how" of redemption is now no longer debated with much passion. These days at the forefront of Christian debates is the "how" of creation, which for centuries had been commonly understood and neglected as a given.

The current debate about creation, which has aroused passionate denunciations and strong animosities, has been caused by the perception that the scientific theory of evolution presents a direct challenge to traditional biblical Christianity. The basis and the contours of this debate have been analyzed already many times and people have taken positions on them. It may legitimately be questioned whether science and faith operate in the same arena, and therefore can challenge and criticize each other. People also debate the significance of specific scientific pieces of evidence, or the over all import of the theory of evolution. Among believers there has been a long standing conversation about the literal and the symbolic value of specific biblical statements. Since I am not a scientist, nor a systematic theologian, I do not intend to enter into these debates.

It seems to me that any one wishing to teach a biblical view of the "how" of creation must take into account the whole Bible, and not arbitrarily limit the evidence to Genesis 1-3, much less to Gen. 1:1-2:4. To limit the biblical evidence to "creation week" is a myopic reduction of the evidence that cannot legitimately be sustained by any one who affirms the Scriptures are the Christian's rule of faith and practice. Unexplainably, however, this has been the case in the debates about creation and evolution

There are those who seem to think that if they find a text of scripture that supports what they wish to believe or do that is all it takes to prove adherence to the Bible. Even if in some quarters until today the "proof-text" method of biblical study is common usage, its inadequacy has been recognized since the end of the eighteenth century. It is, therefore, high time for Christians who claim to be scripturally based to adopt positions on doctrine or morals only after having taken a serious look at all the biblical evidence on the matter. To propound a doctrine based on one text of Scripture, many times taken out of context, is not a responsible way to represent what the Bible teaches. This book is an attempt to give a representative overlook of the biblical evidence about creation so that readers may adopt well-conceived conclusions that are truly biblically based.

An earlier version of the chapters of this book first appeared as monthly columns in www.spectrummagazine.org between July 2010 and May 2011. Those columns have been re-written for this book taking into account the expanded horizon gained once they had all appeared and the different audience this book wishes to address. The re-writing of the columns has benefitted from comments posted by various readers in the web and more specifically by friends and family who read and criticized the early drafts of the revised chapters. I owe much to Jean and Don Rhoads. They saved me from both syntactical and idiomatic malpractice, and from less than clear sentences. Edward W. H. Vick, the author of a companion volume, read my text and checked that we were complementing each other. Terence Martin made many helpful suggestions concerning the implications of what I had written. My sons, Herold and Carlos, and my wife, Aida, also read the drafts, offered helpful suggestions for their improvement and gave me unconditional support. My editor and publisher, Henry Neufeld, merits my special gratitude for having offered me a contract for the publication of a book I had not yet quite written. That was a first for me. He also decided to make this a companion volume to the book by Edward W. H. Vick which takes a look at the Christian doctrine of creation from a systematic perspective. I am most indebted to him for the professionalism and dedication with which he has carried this project to a most satisfying completion.

INTRODUCTION

These days, unfortunately, the United States is divided on a long list of issues. They range from social issues, like abortion and gay marriage, to political issues, like the role of government in the market and the proper use of military power in the territory of other sovereign nations. These issues certainly are very important and the positions adopted on them will make significant differences to the future history of our nation. I fear, however, that another issue that has been pestering our national life for over a century continues to have a significant impact on our society and its effects are increasingly deleterious. I refer to the debate concerning the scientific study of nature and Christian faith. Like the other issues mentioned above, it must be admitted, its importance spills over national frontiers. By referring to its impact on the American horizon, I am in no way saying that it is not also very significant in the lives of Christian believers in other countries.

That nature reveals an evolutionary process is not a recent discovery. The ancient Greeks as early as the third century B.C.E. knew that things in nature evolve. When Charles Darwin became a student at Cambridge University his professors were teaching evolution as a phenomenon clearly visible in nature. Of course, there were also prominent Cambridge theologians who opposed any deviation from a static view of nature. They insisted that nature be taken as a system that began six thousand years ago, as Ussher's chronology of biblical history then being printed on the margins of Bibles told everyone.

Charles Darwin's contribution to modern science was to offer an explanation as to how evolution takes place. He brought out the evidence collected during his three-year-long journey around the world on the *Beagle* to argue that the engine for the evolution of life forms was what he called "natural selection."

Ever since Darwin, biologists have been studying the ways in which living organisms evolve. In the process they have been making modifications to Darwin's explanations. As a result, the notion of natural selection has become a hotly debated issue among biologists. The decipherment of the genome and more generally the rise of genetics as the most rapidly advancing area of biology have made biologists realize that natural selection does not by itself account for all the changes taking place in living organisms. Natural selection is to be seen in conjunction with gene duplication and random (and not so random) mutations as the factors bringing about evolutionary change.

The commanding position of Darwin's theory as the best way to understand how evolution works, however, gave rise to strong opposition to it by those who saw it as a threat to the authority of the Bible. In an effort to sustain belief in the biblical records within a society that was benefiting from the advances of science and their application in technologies that make life more comfortable, fundamentalists came up with creationism. This is an effort to make the creation account of Genesis scientifically valid. Such effort came to a head at a well publicized trial on December 7-9, 1981, at Little Rock, Arkansas. The trial tested the constitutionality of a law passed by the Arkansas legislature. Act 590 required that in every class in science in the school system of this state the "two scientific models" concerning the origin of "the universe, earth, life and man" should receive "balanced treatment." The two models were defined as "creation science" and "evolution science". While it clarified that no religious instruction was allowed in the classrooms, it insisted that the "scientific evidences and the inferences therefrom" were to be presented in favor of both scientific models. The trial resulted in Judge William Overton ruling that "creation-science" is not science but religion. A somewhat related law passed in Louisiana was tested at the Supreme Court of the United States. In the 1987 case *Edwards v. Aguillard* this law was declared unconstitutional. As these efforts by creationists proved unsuccessful and the courts declared that "creation science" was not at all science but religious doctrine, the fundamentalist point of view was renamed "Intelligent Design" in order to obscure its theological underpinnings. This subterfuge, however, has not deceived anyone.

The battle over evolution vs. creationism has been raging in our midst and, unfortunately, it has not been limited to the social gatherings of inquisitive adults. It is being fought in the school boards of the nation and has been having a deleterious effect in the science classrooms not only of our public schools but also in those of some religiously controlled colleges. Many professors in denominational colleges are being asked to offer creationism as a viable scientific alternative to evolution.

It may be argued that the pressure to denigrate scientific findings as "so called science" leaves students with a misunderstanding of science and a low estimate of its benefits. Comparative studies of the knowledge of science among secondary school students in different nations rate American high school students in seventeenth place. As a consequence the population at large is suffering from an ideological misdirection of the educational curriculum. This is particularly true among those who discontinue their formal education with a high school diploma. I think, therefore, that this issue has increasing significance on account of its multiple consequences.

Closer to home, it is to be noted that young people of this generation are growing up with distinctive traits and preferences. They are much less inclined than previous generations to wish to establish their own place under the sun by themselves. The rampant individualism of the near past is giving place to a more community-oriented style of life. But their idea of community is not necessarily institutionalized or ideologically delimited. This means that they are leaving the churches of their parents in large numbers. The Barna Group sponsored a five year study of the reasons young people leave the churches of their childhood. In the book making public the results of this study, *You Lost Me: Why Young Christians are Living Church and Rethinking Church*, David Kinnaman reports that thirty-five percent of the respondents said they resented that Christians are too confident they know all the answers. Twenty-five percent identified Christianity as anti-science as a reason for leaving, and twenty-three percent said they had been turned off by the creation-versus-evolution debate.

Since I am neither a scientist nor a historian or philosopher of science, I do not feel I can contribute to the elucidation of the issues involved in this debate. Even if I were, probably I would not get into the fray after the highly commendable recent contribution by Conor Cunningham. His book, *Darwin's Pious Idea: Why the Ultra-Darwinists and the Creationists Both Get it Wrong,* explains the twists and turns both among Darwinists and creationists through the years with admirable clarity and charts a path for bringing about a *concordat* between the camps. His argument is built on evidence from orthodox Christian theology which the creationists seem to ignore. Still, Cunningham argues, with the creationists, that all the biblical evidence on creation is found in Genesis' first three chapters.

Furthermore, I am fortunate to be writing this book as a companion volume to one by my colleague Edward W. H. Vick. In his book he takes a look at the Christian doctrine of creation within the framework of systematic theology. Thus, I can concentrate my study of creation on the evidence available in the biblical texts. Still, I shall preface my study by some general observations concerning issues that sometimes interfere with the study of the biblical materials.

To affirm that God is the Creator of the heavens and the earth does not require that creationism control what is taught in science classes. To characterize nature as creation is a theological statement. To study nature scientifically is to use the knowledge already attained by evidence objectively studied to predict possible scenarios in areas yet to be studied. On the basis of such predictions, and the theories that support them, scientists design experiments and carry on expeditions to gather evidence and test whether their predictions are correct.

Is it necessary to say that it is impossible to predict possible results and design experiments on the basis of creationism? Creationism is neither theology, i.e., an affirmation of creation as a theological statement, nor is it science. It is an ideology and, like all ideologies, only serves to distract the uninformed and hide the agenda of those who espouse it.

No scientific experiment has ever been designed using the conception of the universe as a three-story building with the earth in the ground floor and the waters in the basement and the upper floor. It is safe to say that none will ever be. Who with open eyes can affirm that the plant and animal species extant are the same ones that were created by God six thousand years ago? What can be predicted and which experiment that advances our knowledge of nature can be designed on the basis of such a postulate? To offer creationism as science is to ignore what scientific theories are for.

All science deals only with theories. Theories provide the structure with which to make predictions and design experiments to test them. That is their function and as such they work well. Of course, as new evidence obtained by such experiments multiplies and knowledge of a particular corner of nature increases, the theory that helped in the process is continuously being adjusted, modified, and perfected. If creationists understood this, they would not wish to offer the Genesis accounts as a scientific structure. Would creationists be willing to adjust the biblical "scientific theory" according to the results of the experiments that may be used to test it? It is precisely because science is this way that atheist, agnostic, Jewish, Moslem, Christian, and other kinds of religious scientists are able to work together harmoniously in the testing and the interpretation of the data made available as science continues its advancement.

Scientists who are Christian have found different ways in which to hold firm their faith in God as Creator while doing their scientific work. Some have decided that the theory of evolution is a frontal attack to the Christian faith and try to find ways by which to interpret the data to harmonize with the biblical accounts of creation. A few have tried to show that the biblical accounts are better scientifically than what is reported on the basis of the theory of evolution. Most observers agree, however, that those taking these views cease to be scientists and have become merely misguided believers.

The evolution of species was recognized by all scientists when Charles Darwin was a university student. The factors influencing the evolution of species were what Darwin studied and what scientists are still studying and will continue to study. On the basis of these studies science has made the advances that have made our lives today much more pleasant than those of our ancestors. As far as I know, no scientific advancement has been achieved on the basis of creationism.

Darwin's main contribution was to note that nature carried on a labor similar to that performed by breeders of pedigreed domestic animals. By selecting members of a species with certain specific characteristics, and selecting their descendants with the desired characteristics over several generations, eventually breeders produce a generation in which all members have the desired characteristics. In this way breeders produce cows, dogs, cats and horses of different breeds. Darwin postulated that a similar process takes place in nature without human intervention. Darwin's observations opened up a way of understanding *how* evolution takes place, they did not show *that* it happens – that was already known. Based on Darwin's observations scientists have made innumerable advances affecting evolution in its multiple aspects. These advances, however, do not detract from the value of Darwin's foundational work.

Every scientist considers Charles Darwin one of the greatest scientists in human history. The British nation, an officially

Christian nation in which the king or queen is the head of both the state and the church, is so proud of him that it has placed his portrait in one of the bills of its currency. With humility I thank Charles Darwin for having made possible the scientific advances that allow me to have lived already seventeen years more than either my father or my mother. I think it is impossible to be a responsible, honest and grateful Christian and not recognize the contributions Charles Darwin made to science. All modern life scientists stand on his shoulders. To deny it is at best ingratitude and at worst either ignorance or hypocrisy. The church may harbor many faults within and survive, but it may not retain these two in these days.

Scientists do not have faith in evolution. Faith is faith, and science is science. Scientists work on the basis of evidence. Those who have evidence do not need faith. Scientific theories are not believed; they are tested. The science laboratories do not provide evidence of the work of God. Scientists who have faith in God the Creator affirm by faith that God is at work in the natural processes they observe in their laboratories. Faith is not the ability to conceptualize. If that were the case, then, as the biblical book of *James* says, the demons have faith in God, and creationists have faith in Satan. Faith has to do with our trust and dependence on a Creator God.

To believe is one thing; to have faith is something else. In practice, the difference between faith in God and scientific belief is that faith, even while standing over against conceptual insecurities, exhibits one hundred per cent certainty. Scientists affirm conclusions on the basis of the preponderance of the evidence, never achieving one hundred per cent certainty. The certainty of faith is neither grounded on scientific knowledge nor on theological beliefs, i.e., freedom of the will. Every statement by a scientist, like the posted price for an airline ticket, is subject to change without notice. No matter how many times they change their minds about specific scientific beliefs, scientists who have faith in God may continue to affirm their trust in The Creator. The same is true of theologians who change their minds about predestination or some other theological belief.

Often one hears creationists charge that evolutionists have faith in science. This means, according to them, that the issue rests on one's decision as to whether to believe the Bible or believe science. The same creationists would also admit that faith and presumption are not quite the same, that in fact presumption is an abuse of faith. To have faith is to trust unconditionally. To have presumption is to assume power and test the one being trusted.

It is obvious that scientists do not have faith. They have presumption. They assume power over the objects of their study and test their theories about the way in which they would behave. Christians have faith in God. Scientists have presumptions on their theories. Creationists don't have faith. Like scientists, they have presumptions. But while scientists can test their presumptions on their theories, creationists cannot test theirs on their ideology.

To learn from Darwin has nothing to do with faith. It only says that one participates in the intellectual life of the twenty-first century. The battle cries shouted by the fundamentalists who pretend to be arbiters of what can be believed or conceptualized by a believing scientist only confirm what accumulated Wisdom teaches: beliefs neither win nor die "with their boots on" in intellectual battle fields. They only die abandoned in nursing homes without relatives who visit or bury them. The future of the seven days of twenty four hours and the six thousand years is the same as that of the flat earth and the geocentric universe, which are also biblical conceptualizations that were once defended and fought for as if Christian faith depended on them. We must all learn the lesson that the invincible war machine of the United States learned in Vietnam. It is impossible to win in the battle field the hearts and minds of those who are defending their fatherland or their freedom of conscience. Creationists who fight battles to defend the scientific validity of the Genesis accounts face a no-win outcome. Ultra Darwinist atheists who wish to defeat creationism make a category mistake misunderstanding the nature of ideologies.

The Bill of Rights issued by the founding fathers of the United States of America declares that "all men are created equal." That is certainly not a scientific statement. We all know that nature endows each of us with attributes in different measures. Some are born with large lung capacities and excellent muscular coordination and reflexes, which allow them to be excellent athletes. Others are born with a lesser measure of this attributes. Some are born with superior powers of concentration and memory, while others suffer from deficiencies in these areas. From the point of view of nature, all men and women are not created equal. Is anyone eager to deny the inequality with which nature "creates" human beings? Is any one eager to have the words in the Bill of Rights discredited as "unscientific"? No one is even thinking of doing such things because every one understands that the founding fathers were making a theological statement. They went on to add: "and are endowed by their Creator with inalienable rights." The founding fathers were making a theological statement about the purpose and value of every human being. We continue to agree with their assessment and therefore consider that the child with severe mental or physical handicaps is just as valuable as the most gifted of our children. Even atheists agree. The same is true of the scientific and the theological ways of looking at the world around us.

I would like to contribute to this divisive issue, but not by engaging in an argument with ultra Darwinists or creationists. I consider myself a person who seeks peace. My contribution is an effort to place on the table the evidence that needs to be taken into account by those who affirm faith in the God of the Bible. Creation is a fundamental theme in the Bible, and faith's affirmations of God's creative action find expression in multiple ways. Creationism, on the other hand, is an ideology that manipulates biblical stories and pretends that they have scientific validity. Creationists and ultra Darwinists who deny the existence of what cannot be the subject of scientific study are involved in a battle that, as I have already said, cannot be won with the boots on.

Most scientists understand the limits of what science can study. I am not in any way wishing to enter the battlefield in which creationists wish to defeat evolution. For creationism I have no use. Given the centrality of the Creator God in the Bible, however, I would like to pay closer attention to what the whole Bible has to say about creation. That is, I do not accept the reductionist way in which the participants in "the battle of the Bible" limit the biblical evidence on creation to what is found in Genesis 1-3.

My aim is to explore what different parts of the Bible say about creation. My exploration does not aim to be exhaustive, but to be representative. I will try, as far as I am able, to bring out what must certainly be considered as the evidence. I leave it to my readers to draw the conclusions they think the evidence supports. Those who claim to form their opinions on the basis of what the Bible teaches cannot ignore most of the evidence and make arguments based on three of its chapters. A debate as divisive as the debate about the relationship of the Bible and science cannot be an honest debate if most of the evidence, whether from science or from the Bible, is overlooked. Thus, rather than entering the debate, I propose to my readers to bracket the debate and examine the biblical evidence as a whole. After the evidence has been duly taken into account, then an unbiased assessment is in order.

In the chapters that follow, each will focus its attention in a biblical book, or on books that belong together. The first section of each chapter will have a brief introduction to the main theme in the text being considered. Then I will try to show the role creation plays within the context of this main theme. Since each book, or cluster of books, deals with specifics at a particular time and participates in a concrete cultural environment, each chapter will try to show how creation within the Bible is viewed in varied and sometimes contrasting ways. By taking seriously the various ways in which creation is viewed within the Bible modern believers should find their warrant to understand creation in the twenty-first century in yet another way. No matter in which way the biblical authors viewed creation, they were free to affirm their faith in the Creator. We, like them, can also affirm our faith in the Creator God no matter how we view the natural world and the universe in which we live. The Bible itself demonstrates the independence of faith from any and all cultural descriptions of the material reality of which we are a part. This is the argument of this book.

Creation in the
Prophetic Literature

In ancient Israel there were both official and charismatic prophets. The official prophets were employed by the court and the temple. The charismatic prophets confronted the throne and the temple with accusations of idolatry and injustice. Idolatry manifested itself both in the importation of foreign gods and in the participation in the fertility cults of Canaan. Military alliances with other nations, according to the prophets, weakened national security instead of guaranteeing it. Thus, marrying foreign princesses as part of foreign policy, and the establishment of temples to their gods was seen by the prophets as a rejection of Yahve. These sanctuaries to foreign gods, together with the high places and the groves where the cult of the fertility deities of Canaan was carried on, attracted the majority of Israelites before the Babylonian exile (605 – 536 B.C.E.).

The prophets also indicted the political powers for prevalent injustice. While the "former" prophets were remembered for their conduct before kings (we may think of Samuel and Elijah in this connection), the prophets whose sayings were valued and preserved addressed the people as interpreters of what was taking place from the perspective of Yahve.

Injustice was manifest in the unequal distribution of wealth. The rich had summer homes and winter homes (Amos 3:15), spent their days eating mutton with an abundance of wine and songs and their nights sleeping in beds of ivory (Amos 6:4-6). In the meantime, the poor wasted their lives in forced labor with little bread and no beds. The greed of the rich is described as the behavior of wild beasts which tear apart and devour weaker animals. In nature might makes right and morality does not exist. In history justice must prevail, and God takes care of its existence. "Hear, you heads of Jacob and rulers of the house of Israel! Is it not for you to know justice? – you who hate the good and love the evil, who tear the skin from off my people, and their flesh from off their bones; who eat the flesh of my people, and flay their skin from off them, and break their bones in pieces, and chop them up like meat in a kettle, like flesh in a caldron. Then they will cry to the Lord, but he will not answer them" (Micah 3:1-4).

The message of the prophets, according to most of their readers, has been encapsulated in other words of Micah:

"With what shall I come before the Lord?
Shall I come before him with burnt offerings?
with calves a year old?

Will the Lord be pleased with thousands of rams?
with ten thousands of rivers of oil?
Shall I give my first-born for my transgression?
the fruit of my body for the sin of my soul?"

He has showed you, O human, what is good;
and what does the Lord require of you
but to do justice,
to value covenant loyalty,
and to live humbly with your God (6:6 – 8).

Here we learn what we must do to stand before God. The religious life is not manifested primarily by participation in the cult, even when it includes extraordinary acts of ritual devotion. The religious life consists of daily living. It is by dealing justly with our neighbors, showing loyalty to the covenant with God, and recognizing God's power and glory by a humble demeanor that we are accepted before Yahve.

The prophets distinguished themselves by their engagement with history. In fact, starting with the first one, Amos (*circa* 750 B.C.E.), they discovered that a person's life does not acquire meaning by being tied to ceremonial rites that are repeated in annual, monthly or weekly cycles. Life acquires meaning as it forges a future, and God is the One who is actively leading His people toward the future. In this way God makes history and human beings occupy it.

The prophets of Israel have the honor of having been the first philosophers of history, the first to break the circularity of traditional societies that identify themselves with a golden past that every succeeding generation is bound to preserve. Amos proclaimed for the first time a "Day of the Lord" (5:18-20). This future day is determinative of the quality of all human life. It is the day of judgment of the nation, the day of the divine verdict on the history of nations.

For the prophets the central idea is the covenant that ties the people to God. The covenant, obviously, is a historical reality. It was established at the Exodus, the clearest manifestation of God's action to forge a people with a historic mission. With the destruction of the temple of Jerusalem in 586 B.C.E., the future of the nation as a viable community was severely tested. As a consequence, the prophets of this period, Jeremiah and Ezekiel, gave to the covenant a more individualistic application.

For the prophets, Yahve is the God of the future. God's promises are an invitation to the future. The prophets struggled to prove that Yahve is not only stronger than the other gods, but in fact that Yahve is the *only* God since the other gods are idols and idols are nothing (Is. 40:19-20; 41:6-7). Isaiah considers that the final proof for his argument is that Yahve of Israel, the creator who is constantly creating both in the cosmos and in history, is the only God who holds the future and, therefore, the only One capable of predicting it (Is. 41:21-24). Being loyal to the covenant opens the future to the people.

The prophets see two very important things in creation: 1) creation identifies the God with whom they are bound by a covenant, and 2) creation is part of the historical reality in which they live, not just an event of a remote past. In the same way in which Yahve is tied to His people by a covenant, God is also tied to creation. The faithfulness with which God creates each new day is the guarantee of his faithfulness to God's people.

For the prophets, nature and history are not two discrete universes with characteristics particular to each, as they are for modern academics. Classical Hebrew did not have words for nature, society, history, or universe. These words name abstract concepts that were unknown to them. The prophets did not distinguish between nature and history. The realm in which Yahve acts is one. Yahve's faithfulness is one and the same in all God's activity.

Jeremiah said it well. He announced that Yahve intended to establish a new covenant which would not be like the covenant made with the fathers. They had broken that covenant and consequently were being taken into exile in Babylon. Jeremiah says, "Thus says the Lord, who gives the sun for light by day and the fixed order of the moon and the stars for light by night, who stirs up the sea so that its waves roar, . . . If this fixed order departs from before me, says the Lord, then shall the descendants of Israel cease from being a nation before me for ever" (Jer. 31:35-36).

According to this declaration, the permanency of Israel as a nation is guaranteed by the permanency of the solar system. History and nature are one and the same realm in which the sovereignty and the fidelity of Yahve are evident. Jeremiah comforted the people of Israel facing exile with the promise of a new covenant. Addressing the power of Yahve, Isaiah asks, "Was it not thou who cut Rahab in pieces, who pierced the dragon? Was it not thou who dried up the sea, the waters of the great deep; who made the depths of the sea a way for the redeemed to pass over?"

(Is. 51:9-10). On the basis of Yahve's performance at creation and the exodus, Isaiah predicts the people's joyful return from exile.

Here creation is described as the cut that severed Rahab into two hemispheres, the thrust that pierced the dragon to death. Both references recall theogonic narratives of neighboring nations. These monsters represented the chaos that needed to be mastered in order to install cosmos. The reference to the crossing of the sea during the exodus also assumes cosmic proportions when the Red Sea becomes "the waters of the great deep". Again we notice that the act that brings the cosmos to existence (cutting Rahab) and the act that brings to existence Israel (cutting the sea) are considered in parallel by the prophet since the Red Sea is part of the waters of chaos on which the earth is founded. Both acts provide the means for identifying Yahve. Isaiah continues asking, "Have you forgotten the Lord, your Maker, who stretched out the heavens and laid the foundations of the earth?" (51:13). God is the God of history who is " Maker" both of God's people and of the heavens and the earth. For Isaiah the union of cosmos and history includes the history of all nations (40:21-23).

While it is true that creation is something God *did* "in days of old, the generations of long ago" (51:9), creation was not *accomplished* then. The One who cut Rahab and pierced the dragon *then* is also the One who creates each passing moment. If night follows day and dawn puts an end to night is because Yahve is actively creating. Yahve is the God who created, formed and made (Is. 43:7), but also the one who now and in the future redeems (Is. 43:1-7). Creation is not *a fait accompli*. It is a *creatio continua*. To put it in contemporary American terms, creation is not a "mission accomplished" Amos puts this notion on relief: "He who made the Pleiades and Orion, and turns deep darkness into the morning, and darkens the day into night, who calls for the waters of the sea, and pours them out upon the surface of the earth, the Lord is his name" (5:8; compare 4:13). The succession of days and nights and the rising and lowering of the tides are to be seen together with the placing of the Pleiades and Orion in the cosmos.

For the prophets cosmos and history are one, but it does not follow on this account that the prophets were interested in the "how" of creation. In fact, as we already saw, when they refer to how it happened they relapse to the mythological language of the cosmogonies known to them. Instead of making reference to a creation week they parade Rahab, Leviathan, the dragon of the sea, and the waters of the deep.

For us the language of mathematics has become the best vehicle to convey our understanding of creation, and with mathematics we are creating (or discovering?) a universe best understood cybernetically. The prophets were the precursors in the transposition of the description of the universe from mythological narratives to the historical existence of Israel. This was a most significant discursive shift. The prophets, as said above, were the discoverers of history as a purposeful divine activity, and they attached creation to it. This transposition of references to creation that ties it to historical events in the life of the people was the first step in the secularization of nature, even if what the prophets considered history is not what we today call history. They were the ones who took away the gods from nature and thereby began the process of secularization. By insisting that human beings must become responsible for their future, the prophets broke the ties that had bound humans to the cycles of nature. As a result, creation became the guarantee of God's faithfulness. Creation became a servant to history.

One of the forms used in the prophetic oracles is what scholars called the "divine lawsuit" (in Hebrew, RIB). In these oracles Yahve announces that God is taking the people to court in order to make charges against them. Of course, at the court the one with a complaint needs witnesses, preferably two in order to establish the validity of the complaint. Characteristic of these "divine lawsuits" is that God presents "the heavens and the earth" as the witnesses that certify the charges being made. In other words, creation is here personified and plays a historical role in court.

The apocalypticists, the heirs of the prophets who rehabilitated the language of mythology, then felt free to predict the destruction of creation and history. They took a major step into the future by distancing the creation from its Creator. According to them God is free to break the covenant with creation and revoke the order of the sun, the moon and the stars. The prophets considered creation God's identity card. The apocalypticists saw it as infected by The Fall. Paul heard it groaning for redemption, but John the theologian saw it ready for destruction. But we must not get ahead of our story.

What is to be taken into account is that the first descriptions of the how of creation in the Bible used the mythological language of the neighboring cultures. To create, Yahve cut Rahab in two, pierced the dragon, put limits to the primordial ocean. But that is not what counts. What counts is that the God of Israel is the creator and sustainer of the natural order in which Israel lives. Since the natural order is firm and sustained by Yahve, the future of Israel is garanteed.

CREATION IN THE WISDOM LITERATURE AND *THE PSALMS*

The Wisdom tradition flourished in Israel among the courtiers and the scribes who worked for the king. As such, those who sought after wisdom were people with social and economic advantages, agents of the king in diplomatic missions and members of the bureaucracy that kept close to the centers of political power. What in the East was called *wisdom* came to be known as *philosophy* in Greece. In its origins wisdom had to do with the behavior to be adopted by those who live the way life should be lived. The sayings of the wise crossed frontiers freely and promoted conservative, stable societies. Their principal theme was not to advise against injustice or idolatry but to exalt material, intellectual and spiritual wealth. The instructions of the wise aimed at advancing the social and economic standing of their disciples. Since God acts according to retributive justice, one is to obey the rules of the dominant social culture so that "you may prosper in the land."

Even if in Israel "the fear of the Lord" was considered "the beginning of wisdom" and it was to have priority over the social culture, most of the proverbs of the wise had a secular perspective and could have been taught in any of the neighboring nations. Proverbs similar to those found in the Bible are also found in the wisdom traditions of Egypt, Babylon and Canaan. It is notable that in the wisdom literature of the Old Testament, Israel is not singled out as exceptional; no mention is made of Israel's election or of the covenant that distinguishes it among the nations. The prophets and Deuteronomy give *chesed*,[1] a very rich word which also means "covenant loyalty," priority among God's attributes. With this meaning it does not appear in the wisdom books, but does in the Psalms.

The biblical wisdom literature is also notable because while one learns in it how to prosper and maintain the *status quo*, one also finds in it critics who question popular belief, who do not submit to the authority of the elders. The book of *Proverbs* teaches how to make friends, make money and have influence in the community. In *Ecclesiastes* we find an author, Qoheleth (Eccl. 12:11),[2] who examines the instructions of the wise and the folly of fools and determines that "wisdom excels folly as light excels darkness. The wise man has his eyes in his head, but the fool walks in darkness; and yet I perceived that one fate comes to all of them" (Eccl. 2:13-14). In other words, at the end there is no difference between them. Death is the ultimate equalizer.

Qoheleth admonishes the one going to the house of God to draw near to listen rather than to offer the sacrifice of fools "who do not know that they are doing evil . . . . When you vow a vow to God, do not delay paying it; for he has no pleasure in fools" (Eccl. 5:1, 4). In both cases what is to be avoided is not to act unjustly or to be idolatrous; it is to be a fool. Surely this advice could have been given in any religious context.

The application of wisdom is universal. On account of it, "There is nothing better for a man than that he should eat and drink, and find enjoyment in his toil. This also, I saw, is from the hand of God" (Eccl. 2:24). Life is to be lived to the fullest now. The one thing that counts is to have "enjoyed life's good things" (Eccl. 6:3, 6).

---

1   *chesed* ranges in meaning from "rock," "fortress" to "mercy," tender mercy."

2   This Hebrew designation is somewhat elusive. English Bibles designate him "the Preacher" or "the Teacher." Ecclesiastes is the name given to him in the Greek translation of the Hebrew text, the Septuagint (LXX).

As a true philosopher, Qoheleth is a liberal, a critic of the constrictions imposed by a society that exalts traditional values. While he would like to use pleasing words, as a good Shepherd he speaks words that are "like goads, and like nails firmly fixed" (Eccl. 12:10-11). In this he is not much different from Socrates. He admonishes his young disciples: "Rejoice, O young man, in your youth, and let your heart cheer you in the days of your youth; walk in the ways of your heart and the sight of your eyes. But know that for all these things God will bring you into judgment . . . . remember also your Creator in the days of your youth" (Eccl. 11:9, 12:1). Thus, while recognizing the seriousness of God's final judgment, he trusts the intelligence of the young and allows them freedom to follow their own judgment in their everyday life. That is the hallmark of liberalism.

For the wise, the human family lives under their Creator, and the Creator is God Almighty. Because of his incomprehensible experience, Job can imagine a god who is unjust, but cannot conceive a God who is not almighty. Precisely because God is The Almighty, and in God's creation retributive justice does not work, since evidently the wicked prosper and the righteous suffer, according to Job, God is neither loving nor just. For the author of *Job*, however, creation demonstrates that God is almighty and that human beings must recognize the distance that separates the One who inhabits eternity from those who live on earth where everything is transitory.

As Qoheleth said, God "has made everything beautiful in its time; also he has put eternity into man's heart, yet so that he cannot find out what God has done from the beginning to the end" (Eccl. 3:11). "God is in heaven, and you upon earth" (Eccl. 5:2). "I know that whatever God does endures forever; nothing can be added to it, nor anything taken from it; God has made it so, in order that men should fear before him" (Eccl. 3:14).

Based on this premise of Qoheleth, the author of *Job* has God finally confronting Job to make him confess that, since he had nothing to do with creation and God is the Almighty Creator, Job must follow the advice of Qoheleth, speaking less and listening more. Wrapped in the whirlwind God accuses Job of speaking words without knowledge (Job 38:2). With patent sarcasm God asks Job to give details about creation, assuming that one who considers himself sufficiently wise to accuse God of injustice should have such information. By making Job aware of his ignorance about creation God takes away the wind from under Job's wings, just as he was haughtily proclaiming his sinlessness. Now Job admits, "Behold, I am of small account; what shall I answer thee? I lay my hand on my mouth. I have spoken once . . . twice, but I proceed no further" (Job 40:4-5).

Creation and its mysteries belong only to God. The theology of the wise men of Israel in its entirety is based on creation, not on election and covenant as events in history. Their theology embraces the whole human family; it is universal. It emphasizes, however, that the truly wise person admits ignorance about the details of creation. Human beings must recognize themselves as creatures within God's creation. Only then may they attain wisdom. Then the fear of Yaveh is the beginning of wisdom.

The authors of *Ecclesiastes* and *Job* provide sharp criticism of the parochial theology of Deuteronomic orthodoxy where God's approval is measured by the family's wealth. They criticize the promoters of orthodoxy who pretend to know much, talk folly and offer sacrifices without knowing that they do evil.

The legendary story at the beginning and the end of the book of *Job* contains dialogues constructed to serve the agenda of the book. They are not transcripts of conversations taking place in the council of the sons of God, or in the house where Job suffered his boils, or of a confrontation between a God wrapped in a storm and Job. The book is a theological work of the first magnitude in which we are admonished not to confuse a god created by human attempts to explain things with the God who is the Creator of heaven and earth. On the basis of the god of Deuteronomic orthodoxy, which the author of *Job* rejects, Job accused God of being unjust. Confronted by the Almighty Creator God Job declares himself unworthy (something which in his long dispute with his friends he adamantly had refused to do) and seats himself "in dust and ashes" (Job 42:6). The drama of *Job* teaches us that the Creator God is not the one that human beings construct to satisfy psychological needs or theological expediencies (Job 42:3, 5).

The psalmists share with the wise a profound admiration for the power of the Almighty Creator God. For them, also, the Almighty has triumphed over the forces of chaos that ruled in the darkness of the abyss and has established cosmos, order and beauty. God has imprisoned under lock and key those opposing forces and has established for them limits which they cannot trespass (Job 7:12; 26:10 -13; 38:8 - 11; Ps. 104:9; Prov. 8:29).

To gain this victory over chaos, like the prophets and the wise men, the psalmists fall back on the mythological cosmogonies of antiquity. Rahab, Leviathan, the dragon of the sea and the waters of the abyss, which in the time of chaos before creation were over the mountains but now are under control and cannot go beyond their limits (Ps. 104:6-9), appear as significant protagonists in the creation. No human being can place a ring in the nose of Behemoth or of Leviathan and take them around as if they were a domesticated bull. But God who made them both undoubtedly can (Job 40:19; 41:2). God is the one who pierced the twisting serpent (Job 26:13) which needed to be defeated for creation to take place.

The representation of the forces of chaos as having been domesticated by Almighty God reaches its zenith in a Leviathan created by God to play in the sea with the waves, as if it were God's pet (Ps. 104:26). In *Job,* God challenges Job to compare himself with Behemoth, "the most excellent of the works of God" to which God gave authority (a sword) over everything on earth. Its strength is put in relief by a tail like a cedar and genitals with interlaced nerves (Job 40:15-19). In this way Job's impotence is ridiculed by comparison with the strength of Behemoth. Of course, these images of Leviathan in the sea and Behemoth on land contradict the apocalyptic vision of Isaiah 27:1: "In that day the Lord with his hard and great and strong sword will punish Leviathan the fleeing serpent, the twisting serpent, and he will slay the dragon that is in the sea." Leviathan here is no pet splashing in the waves. The positive portrayals of Behemoth and Leviathan in the wisdom tradition underline its optimistic perspective on creation.

Finally, we must take a look at creation in Prov. 8:22 - 31. These verses are, in the first place, an encomium to wisdom and may be divided in three sections: the priority of wisdom among created things (vv. 22-26), the participation of wisdom in creation (vv. 27-30a), and the joy which wisdom has in God and creation, which is reciprocated by the joy God has in wisdom (vv. 30b-31).

The first section establishes the priority of wisdom using a formula that is also used at the beginning of the *Enuma Elish* (the Babylonian creation myth) and at the beginning of the narrative in Gen. 2:4b – 4:26. My purpose in quoting the following texts is only to highlight that all three use the same formula in order to establish the time when creation took place.

Enuma Elish begins by saying:

> When on high the heavens had not been named,
> the earth beneath had not been called by name,
> when primordial Apsu, their begetter
> and Mummu-Tiamat, she bore them all,
> their waters mingled as a single body,
> no reed hut had sprung forth
> no marshland had appeared,
> none of the gods had been brought into being,
> and none bore a name, and no destinies determined,
> then, it was that the gods were formed in the midst of heaven.

Genesis 2:5 says:

> When no plant of the field was yet in the earth
> and no herb of the field had yet sprung up
> for the Lord God had not caused it to rain upon the earth,
> and there was no man to till the ground; . . .
> then, the Lord God formed man of dust from the ground.

Proverbs 8:22-26 says:

> The Lord created me at the beginning of his work,
>   the first of his acts of old.
> Ages ago I was set up, at the first,
>   before the beginning of the earth.
> When there were no depths I was brought forth,
> when there were no springs abounding with water.
> Before the mountains had been shaped,
> before the hills, I was brought forth;
> before he had made the earth with its fields,
> or the first of the dust of the world.

While the author of *Job* points out that Job had not been present at creation and therefore lacks the wisdom necessary to judge God (his judgment having been based on the god of orthodoxy), the author of *Proverbs* points out that wisdom came to be before creation and was present at creation. The syntax of the passage is a bit elusive and makes it difficult to decide whether wisdom was 1) the master craftman, 2) the architect, 3) the magician who carried out the project, or 4) the personification of a divine hypostasis, only present as a witness to creation. But in Prov. 3:19 it is clear that wisdom is considered the agent of creation: "The Lord by wisdom founded the earth; by understanding he established the heavens." This is different, however, from what is said by the psalmist: "By the word of the Lord the heavens were made, and all their host by the breath [spirit] of his mouth" (Ps. 33:6).

The author of *Proverbs*, like the author of Psalm 33 and that of Genesis 1, already conceives God as One inhabiting eternity wholly beyond the imagination of human beings. God is a transcendent being. To carry out creation God utilized the service of a mediating agent, a *demiurgos*. In Prov. 8 the creating agent is wisdom, understanding. For the psalmist it is the word, the spirit. Centuries later, Christians took both of these texts as definitions of the Christ and said that the agent of creation had been the pre-existent Christ.

In the IV century Arius and his followers, on the basis of Prov. 8:30, insisted that the pre-existent Christ was not co-eternal with the Father, since the text says that wisdom came forth as an emanation conceived by the Father that was then used as the master craftsman, the architect of creation.

Even though Prov. 8 is not a poetic narrative of creation, it does give some details of Wisdom's creative activity. The formation of the heavenly dome and of the ocean that is below and around the earth, the stabilization of the dome and of the fountains of the abyss, the setting of limits to the sea and the formation of the subterranean mountains that uphold the disc of the flat earth are to be credited to her. For this work wisdom availed itself of a compass, as a good master craftsman would. The psalmist, on the other hand, describes this work very succinctly: "For he has founded it [the earth] upon the seas, and established it upon the rivers" (Ps. 24:2).

Finally, as in Job 38:7, the wise man of Prov. 8 reminds his disciple that the participants in creation jointly celebrated with joy the completion of the enterprise (v. 31).

In summary, the wise men of Israel emphasize that he who pretends to know how God does things is a fool who speaks in terms of gods created by human beings to satisfy their own needs. He who has confronted the Creator places his hand over his mouth and listens. He does not talk. Wisdom consists in recognizing that God did not place the world within one's grasp from the beginning until the end. In order to say this, the wise and the psalmists of Israel used a cosmological geography that can only be classified as "primitive", and "outdated". Behemoth, Leviathan, Rahab, the dome over a flat earth that floats over the waters secured by mountains with foundations in the abyss cannot be taken seriously today as descriptions of creation. But, then, the wise of ancient Israel recognized that the ways in which they talked about creation were culturally conditioned and therefore warned against pretending to know God's ways. Would that all serious readers of the Bible would heed this wise counsel.

CREATION IN *GENESIS* 2:4B – 4:26

Traditionally the first section of this text has been understood as giving details left unattended in the sketchy presentation of creation in Chapter One. This way of reading also assumes that the whole of the Pentateuch was written by Moses in the XV century B.C.E. Such a reading is still defended by fundamentalists, but cannot stand before the evidence in the text. For more than two centuries biblical scholars have been constructing a broad consensus about sources for the Pentateuch. It holds that the sources were edited several times before they took the form we now read.

The final editorial work was carried out by priests of the Second Temple between 450 – 400 B.C.E. The literary sources used by the editors contained different versions of the same events as well as narratives peculiar to one tradition. In *Genesis, Exodus* and *Numbers* the editors were primarily dependent on two sources, while a third one, less extensively used, can also be identified in sections of the text. To identify these sources scholars study the vocabulary, the name given to God, the names of significant places, the literary style, the identities of the actors, the theological point of view, the metaphors used to describe the relationship of God with Israel, etc.

The editors used their sources mostly in two ways. Sometimes they placed one after the other repeating the same event from two points of view, as is the case with creation. Other times, two or three sources are interlaced into one running narrative, as is the case with the flood. A notable and concise example of the presence of three versions of the same event is found in Moses' three ascents to Mount Sinai in Ex. 24:9-17. In vv. 9-11, Moses, Aaron, Nadab, Abihu and seventy elders climb to the top of the mount where they are met by God. They all sit down to eat and drink and no calamity falls on those celebrating the occasion with God. In vv. 12-14, Moses and Joshua rise and ascend the mountain. Aaron and Hur are left in charge of the affairs of the people below. In vv. 15-17, Moses climbs Mount Sinai alone and spends six days seeing nothing while enveloped in a cloud. On the seventh day the glory of God comes down on the mount and calls Moses while he still sees nothing. At the foot of the mountain the people see a consuming fire at the top of the mount.

Just taking into account two of the criteria mentioned earlier, the name given to God (and God's characteristics) and the identity of the actors, we notice striking differences. In vv.9 – 11 seventy four persons meet, eat and drink with God, thus implying an anthropomorphic God who walks and has intercourse with human beings on earth. In vv. 15 – 17 Moses climbs the mountain alone and a cloud makes invisible the glory of God on the mountain for six day. On the seventh day, a voice speaks to Moses. What the voice said is not reported. In the meantime the people at the foot of the mountain see on its top a devouring fire. In vv. 12 – 14 Moses and Joshua climb the mountain, while Aaron and Hur are left in charge of solving any problems raised by the elders of the people. It would appear that the anthropomorphic God of Israel of vv. 9 – 11 fits well with the God of Gen. 2:4b – 4:26, and the absent Lord of vv. 15 – 17 fits well with the Lord of Gen. 1:1 – 2:4a. Besides, the time reference to six days and a seventh day that makes the difference also appears in both texts.

In the previous chapter about Creation in the Wisdom Literature, I pointed out that Gen. 2:5 uses a formula that is also used by the author of the *Enuma Elish* and the author of Prov. 8:22-31. It singles out things that are now taken for granted and says that we need to envision the time before such things were there. This formula alone should let the reader know that what follows is an independent story of creation. Actually, to describe it at all as a story of creation is somewhat of an overstatement. The story takes into account a very limited horizon. The earth as a whole and the starry heavens are not considered. The visual angle is minimal and parochial.

The story is concerned with the creation of man, and the way in which God attends to his needs. It begins with the creation of the male human. The trees of the garden were already there for his benefit. Animals are then created also for his benefit. It could even be said that man helps in their creation because by naming them he assigns peculiar characteristics to each. God then creates Woman to end man's loneliness. As such, this story reflects a patriarchal, androcentric society. Recognizing this slant in the text, which is an obvious reflection of its historical setting in antiquity, does not in any way require that those taking the Bible seriously impose patriarchal, male-centered societies on the twenty-first century. Neither does it *a priori* disqualify a feminist interpretation of the text. My reading takes the text literally in a manner consonant with historical and linguistic canons.

In this story God is identified by a proper name, YHVH (Yahve). God's ways are quite normal and familiar. It is normal for God to walk on earth and do things human beings often do. God kneads mud and gives it a human form. Not only are humans made with mud but all beasts of the field and all birds of the air are also made from mud. God opens the thoracic cavity of man in order to extract a rib and closes it. Before the creation of man God had planted a garden "in Eden, to the East." This is an immanent God who does not need help from wisdom, the word, or an angel as assisting agents, master workmen, or artificers of creation. This God does what needs to be done personally: kneads mud, cuts ribs, plants trees and walks around the garden searching for disobedient creatures.

In Eden there was a river that watered the garden. It had four tributaries. The descriptions given to the branches make it possible to identify two of them as the Tigris and the Nile. One is called the Euphrates. The other, called Pison, could be the Orontes. The two named first in the text flow into the Mediterranean and the last two into the Persian Gulf. That is, creation is limited to what we know as the Fertile Crescent of the Near East. It goes up the rivers of Mesopotamia, swings east and then south along Lebanon and Canaan and continues further south up the Nile valley. At the center of this semi-circle is the Arabian desert, but the fertile lands along the four rivers have been the cradle of the great ancient civilizations of Babylon, Nineveh, Syria, Tyre and Egypt.

Yahve, who planted a garden and watered it with a river with four branches, gets characterized not only by getting dirty with mud and blood but also by a lack of foreknowledge. God faces unanticipated problems and has to experiment with various options before coming up with the appropriate response. Apparently, God is not omniscient. When God discovers that it is not good for man to be alone, God tries to solve the problem creating animals that could provide him company. When God discovers that none of the animals is what man really needs, God decides to create the woman to be his counterpart.

Now man and woman can, cleaving together, become "one flesh." In this way the race of mortal human beings may survive. Not long afterwards, Adam and Eve discover their nakedness, and God has to devise some clothing and expel them from the garden God had taken much effort to set them up and provide for their needs. But God's plan has been derailed by God's creatures. The God we meet here has the limitations that characterize human beings.

All the trees planted in the Garden of Eden were "pleasant to the sight and good for food" (2:9). Besides these, God also planted two special trees: the tree of life and the tree of the knowledge of good and evil. While all other trees, as suppliers of beauty and fruit, provided for the nourishment of man, woman and the animals, the tree of life and the tree of the knowledge of good and evil fulfilled special functions. Their presence in the garden was specifically only for the benefit of human beings. One was to provide life, and the other to test obedience. They were the links that were to keep human beings subjected to their Creator.

Before the creation of the animals and of woman, God introduced man into the garden to cultivate it and informed him that he could eat of all the trees freely except the fruit of the tree of knowledge. That is, when the only things in existence were the garden with its trees, the river that watered it with its four branches and the man, God introduced a commandment that tells us the purpose for which man was created. He had been created to obey God's command. The day you eat of the fruit of the tree of knowledge, God tells Adam, "you will die" (2:17).

This text tells us that the human beings created by God were, by nature, mortal. They would live as long as they had access to the tree of life. But this access was conditioned on their obedience. If they ate of the fruit of the tree of knowledge they would irremediably die on account of their mortal nature. This reading is corroborated by the climax of the story. The penalty for having eaten the forbidden fruit is not death. It is denial of access to the tree of life. Not able to eat of this fruit, their lives continued their normal course and eventually died.

In this story the tree of life and the tree of knowledge fulfill the function of the temple in other stories of creation. It is intentional to state that these trees were "at the center of the garden" (2:9). These trees were Eden's umbilical cord. By means of these trees Adam and Eve were in contact with the source of life as long as they carried on the purpose for which they had been created. Their obedience to the divine commandment kept them alive and "clothed in innocence." Of course, this condition can only be recognized by those who have already lost it and feel guilty.

In truth, the story of Gen. 2:4b – 4:26 does not deal with the physical or functional reality of creation. Its interest is to consider the nature of human beings and the conditions under which they were intended to live. Its perspective is anthropocentric. Its content emphasizes a change in the relation between God and human beings. The centrality of obedience to a commandment also makes clear that human beings were created with the freedom to disobey. Under such conditions, repeatedly God has to put in place "Plan B."

As already said, according to this story human beings depended on the fruit of the tree of life to live. This tells us that in themselves they were mortal. That death is a possibility does not make their death necessary. A hypothetical question worthy of consideration is: If Adam and Eve had been created immortal, would it have been necessary to plant the tree of life at the center of the garden? I think the answer is "no." By disobeying they did not lose the immortality they did not have. They lost access to the tree of life on which they depended for the continuation of their lives.

This is also demonstrated by the temptation offered by the serpent. Gods, obviously, are immortal. By offering them to become like gods who know good and evil, the serpent offered to transform them into immortals. The temptation consisted in reaching out to become something they were not, to become like immortal gods. The temptation was to escape the condition of mortal beings in which they had been created.

In the early centuries or our era Christian theologians decided that The Fall consisted in the loss of immortality and that creation had been *ex nihilo* and *ab initio temporis*. These notions, however, emerged to answer questions raised by later generations. The first formula says that God was not dependent on existing matter in order to create. God created "from nothing." The second affirms that creation took place at the beginning of time. That is, creation did not exist in God's mind before it became an objective reality. This was a way of saying that the accounts of creation in Genesis are not like the myths of the pagans which describe the activities of the gods in times prior to creation. It also affirms, of course, that time was created when the sun and the moon were created in order to measure it.

The story we are reading is not preoccupied with such issues. More sophisticated theological discourse, aware of the distinctions made by Greek philosophy, finds consideration of such issues unavoidable. According to our story, what was lost was access to the tree of life, not immortality. Before creation there already existed a desert with little humidity, and both human beings and animals came from the dust of that primordial desert, not "from nothing."

Human beings have within themselves a sense of guilt. The knowledge of innate culpability also appears in other stories of creation. In the *Enuma Elish* creation takes place after a cosmic battle of the gods against their widowed mother and her lover. Human beings receive life from the blood of Kingu, who is identified as the leader of the rebellion against Tiamat and Apsu. Kingu is "the guilty one" and human beings received their life from his blood. It is not difficult to understand why human beings who received life from the blood of "the guilty one" now have an innate sense of guilt. Also to be noticed is that in the *Enuma Elish* blood is the depository of life. Thus, in order to give life to humans one must supply the blood by dying. This notion is central to the Bible as well.

The story of human origins in Gen. 2 - 4 takes a monumental theological step forward by abandoning the notion that human life, or the matter with which human beings were made, was derived from gods who have been killed. Here Adam is mud shaped in the form of a human body, and he receives life by the breath (spirit) of God. The materiality of God's living breath is not at the level of the blood of a dead god, and no death takes place in order to bring about new life. Here Behemoth, Leviathan, the dragon or the primordial ocean do not appear. This difference is what the Fathers of the Church in the first centuries of our era tried to affirm by declaring that creation had been *ex nihilo* and *ab initio temporis*. They recognized that the story was trying hard to break away from traditional mythologies. While in many ways it succeeds in its efforts, we can see that it remains bound by the limitations of its own cultural place and time.

The tree of life and the tree of knowledge at the center of the garden were the temple of Eden. They made possible and maintained the pleasant and beautiful life enjoyed by human beings who carried out the purpose of their creation. It is indeed quite appropriate that trees should be the temple of a cosmos that is just a garden. While in other stories humans are created to make possible the leisure of the gods by serving them, and to offer sacrifices of blood to nourish them, in this account humans are created to obey Yahve. In Eden Yahve issued the first commandment: "Do not attempt to be more than what I created you to be. If you pretend to be more, you will cease being."

It is amazing that the first death among human beings was not a death that resulted from the unavailability of the tree of life. It was a death caused by the murder of Abel. Here we find ourselves again before an unforeseen event. Instead of accepting God's advice and relenting from his anger, jealousy overtakes Cain, and he kills his brother. In this way we are alerted with strident cries that there is something in humans that brings about dire consequences and makes for life "East of Eden" to be prone to tragedy. Chapter 4 gives us the genealogy of Cain up to the introduction of music, metallurgy and cities. It ends with Lamech, the second assassin. Once again, God has to implement Plan B, and as a result Adam and Eve have a son, Seth, who takes the place of Abel.

As mortal beings we humans have a paradox at our core: we have both the elusive divine breath that gave us life, and the desire to be more than what our vocation intends. As a consequence, lacking access to the tree of life we become assassins who take the life of others. Considering the nature and the condition of human beings, the authors of this narrative place before us a mirror in which to see ourselves and feel an urge to reflect. As theology, this narrative has relevance for all human beings at all times.

We may be excused for thinking, at times, that this patriarchal, parochial and anthropomorphic story belongs to a time when people had a much simpler life, a much less informed understanding of the physical universe, and lacked the wisdom gained from thousands of years of historical experience. These observations may very well be true, but dismissing this creation narrative on their account would be a grave mistake. We continue to live burdened with guilt in an anthropocentric, jealous manner. As a consequence, there are many moments in our lives when we need an anthropomorphic God who walks on earth always predisposed to punish our disobedience as well as to seek another way (Plan B) to accomplish God's purposes.

CREATION IN GENESIS 1:1 – 2:4A

While Gen. 2:4b – 4:26 is a narrative with a plot and believable actors, Gen. 1:1 – 2:4a is not. The narrative flow that characterizes Gen. 2 - 4 is absent in Gen. 1. Its architectonic structure makes for notable rigidity. It is like a building which has the scaffolding used for its construction still visible. The formulas that sustain the presentation are monotonously repeated: "And God said," "And it was so", "And God called it 'thus'", "And God saw that it was good", "And it was evening and morning of day . . ." Even though these formulas are tied to days in time, they make it appear as though creation were taking place outside of time. This is reinforced by a God who pronounces the creative words without making an appearance. One gets the impression that the authors are fleshing out the formula of Ps. 33:6, "By the word of the Lord where the heavens made and all the host of them . . . ."

Much theology has been made about the use of the Hebrew verb *bara'* to describe the creation. Some scholars have argued that it indicates a creation *ex nihilo*. Others argue that it does not refer to the creation of material things, but to the assigning of functions to materials that were already in existence. This verb appears many times in the Old Testament, and in every case the subject of the sentence is God. On account of this, it has been said that the author is describing a creative activity that is of a different kind and superior to any human creation. That this creation is different is without question, even if in this creation the primordial sea is essential, and therefore, it does not come "out of nothing." That the verb *bara'* carries a special theological stamp is quite doubtful because the author also uses the verbs "made" (1:7, 16, 25, 26, 2:2, 3), "separated" (1:7), "called" (1:5, 8, 10) and "set" (1:17), and in Gen. 2:3 uses "created and made" as synonyms in an epexegetical construction. The evidence, therefore, does not support the notion that *bara'* has a special theological meaning, or that it does not have to do with the creation of matter.

Returning to the structure of the presentation, it has been noted that the sequence raises some questions. Two of the most obvious have been: How could there have been night and day on the first day without the solar system? and how could there have been plants on the third day without the photosynthesis made possible by solar light? The second question, obviously, arose from the discovery of photosynthesis in modern times.

The first one was already taken up in antiquity. Jesus' contemporary Philo of Alexandria noted that the light of the first three days was a supernatural, primordial light. For Philo, this primordial light is the light that shines on every Sabbath, making each one of them a special day. The primordial luminosity that does not depend on the sun is the luminosity of the "Sabbath candles" Jews light up every Friday at sunset. The apostle Paul also alludes to that primordial light as the one that shines in the hearts of believers who receive "the light of the knowledge of the glory of God in the face of Christ" (2 Cor. 4:6). John the Theologian tells us that in the New Earth there will be neither sun nor moon and the primordial light of the first three days will light the lives of the redeemed (Rev. 21:23). In reality, the questions mentioned above reveal that those raising them have not entered the theological space created by the text of Gen. 1. The text should not be expected to address questions that arise from knowledge acquired at a much later time.

A close look at the structure of Genesis 1 shows that its presentation is more tied to time than to space. It begins with the creation of a day and culminates with the creation of the holy and blessed day. In other words, a theology of the Sabbath determines the structure. Here creation and Sabbath are theologically tied.

Since the eighteenth century it has been noted that the first six days are divided in two sequences of three days each. In the first three God creates three environments, or houses, and in the second three God creates the corresponding inhabitants. The second three are related to the first three so that the fourth corresponds to the first, the fifth to the second and the sixth to the third. On the first day, creating light and separating it from darkness, God creates a day. In the fourth day, the sun, the moon and the stars inhabit the night and the day. On the second day God creates the blue dome of heaven and separates the waters, placing some of them above the dome in order to make rain possible. Effectively, God has created the airy space between the waters above and the waters below. On the fifth day God creates the birds of the air and the fish of the waters. On the third day God gathers the waters below to cause the appearance of dry land and makes vegetation cover the earth. On the sixth day God creates land animals, including humans, and gives them vegetation as food.

The logic of this structure, surely, is not that of a scientist. It is that of a theologian. In the earliest version of the Ten Commandments, found in Deuteronomy 5, the Sabbath rest is to remind the people that they had been slave laborers in Egypt, and God had given them rest from their labors. Here the Sabbath rest commemorates a historical event. By linking the Sabbath to creation this account transfers its significance from a historical to a cosmic setting, where it has a much firmer foundation. While history is contingent and capricious, as far as the ancients could tell the cosmos is stable and permanent.

This structure also fulfils polemical needs against the fertility cults that were prevalent among the Israelites before the Exile. By not telling a story, as all other creation narratives in antiquity did, the author is making a compelling effort to transcend those myths. In spite of his efforts in this direction, however, some mythical remnants are noticeable. In verse 2, the pairs "the darkness and the deep" as well as "the formless and the void" remind us of the complementary or contrasting pairs of gods present in ancient creation stories. These theogonic pairs constitute the pantheon. Along these lines, our curiosity is also awakened by the reference to the wind that blows over the sea. Is this a reference to a warm breeze that incubates the sea, or a reference to the wind that must put down a tempestuous sea that refuses to be controlled by the creating Will? The notion that something must be done to the sea before the Creator can carry out the task at hand also appears in ancient creation myths and in the prophetic and wisdom books. It is noteworthy that in Gen. 2 the sea is not mentioned, and instead of depending on the sea God depends on the primordial dusty ground of a waste land to provide the basic stuff for the creation of living things.

Also surprising is that in Gen. 1, even though provision had been made for rain with the water deposits above the heavenly dome (see Gen. 7:11-12), on the third day the vegetation comes forth without the benefit of rain. In the fertility cults rain had singular importance (recall Baal, the Canaanite god of the thunderstorms), but here, obviously polemically, rain plays no role at all. Even if the absence of the sea in Gen. 2, and the absence of rain in Gen. 1 are "arguments from silence," these silences have a very strong voice. They tell us that the biblical authors were consciously engaged in a polemic against mythological polytheism.

The authors show a very strong hand by the way in which they marginalize the sun and the moon, which were foundational divinities in the mythologies of the surrounding nations. These celestial bodies are denigrated by leaving them nameless. God names the darkness "night" and the light "day." God names the space between the waters "heaven." God names the gathered waters below "seas," and what then appears God names "earth". The sun and the moon are left without a name. They are described as the "the greater light" and "the lesser light." How insulting. What does not have a name has no power. These luminaries have a very secondary role. They do not create time. They are the means for measuring it (1:14). Their function is not to rule the destinies of human beings, as astrologers pretended. They only facilitate the adoration of God at the proper time: weekly, monthly and yearly. In this way the polemical intention of the authors who are combating the mythologies of their contemporaries becomes clear.

The creation of human beings gets special handling. In the *Enuma Elish* the gods also consult among themselves before taking this important step. They understand that they are about to make an important decision with strong repercussions. By contrast, in Gen. 1 the "counsel of the sons of God" of which we read in *Job* and in the *Psalms* is left unmentioned. The declaration "Let us make man (sic) in our image, according to our likeness" is what remains of a narrative that told what went on at the council of the sons of God when this decision was made. The declaration quotes only what the divine council decided after some deliberation. It fails to hide completely its polytheistic background but shows unmistakably the polemical thrust of the authors.

What is most notable, however, is that human beings were not created to serve the gods, as in the *Enuma Elish,* or to obey God, as in Gen. 2:4b – 4:26. They were created, male and female together, to represent the absent God within creation. They were created "in the image" of God. Like the image of Nebuchadnezzar that the Israelites in Babylon, together with all Babylonians, were instructed to worship, the image of God on earth was placed to represent God and rule over the other creatures. Every thing created was subjected to the dominion of the representative of God. The image takes the place of and makes present the God it represents, and must be respected as such. Human beings do not have the image stamped on them. They do not carry it. They do not reflect it. They *are* the image of God in creation. It is difficult to imagine a more sublime conceptualization of the vocation of humanity.

Finally, God rests, sanctifies and blesses the seventh day. In this way this creation account culminates, as all creation stories do, with the creation of the temple that gives permanence to what has been created by serving as the umbilical cord between the transcendent God who does not dwell in space and God's creation within time

and space. Temples are microcosms of the cosmos. The temple in
this case is in time. It is a temple supremely appropriate to those
who live in exile or dispersed among the nations. As a memorial
of the liberation from forced labors in Egypt attained at the
Exodus (Deut. 5), the Sabbath already existed in Israel before the
Exile. The priestly tradition within the Pentateuch reaches its
highest theological expression when it gives the Sabbath a cosmic
foundation. In this way, also, the transcendent God who remains
absent from and independent of creation is present within creation
in the Sabbath.

With the exception of fundamentalists, Old Testament scholars
agree that this presentation of creation is one of the last texts of
the Pentateuch to be written, and that it reflects the wisdom that
made it possible for a people with a long history, most of which
was lived among peoples of other races and cultures, to survive
with their identity intact. Their temple, their cosmic center, their
bridge to eternity and their sign of identity is fixed in time. The
sanctification of the Sabbath made their survival possible in spite
of the vicissitudes of their history.

Is it necessary to say that the presentation of creation in Gen.
1:1 – 2:4a is not an official eye-witness report of creation?
Obviously, it is not that. Neither is it a functional or symbolic
representation of reality. It must be read literally for what it is: an
admirable monotheistic theological declaration that denies a
material connection between God and creation, or that nature has
divine powers. The secularization of nature is necessary to
understand the God who transcends nature, and therefore is the
only God worthy of adoration. The Creator of creation is not the
god of this or that natural force but of everything that is. The link
that relates the Creator to creation is the powerful and effective
word of God. The creative word that is alive and active links the
Creator to the creation, but does not establish a material
connection. This is another very significant theological step
forward taken in the Old Testament.

The faith of those who understood this did not need supports or material scaffoldings. The identification of human beings as the representatives of God, as the ones who are God's image, is basic to our understanding of our responsibility toward creation and before God. This is theology with which one can live assured of one's value before God, and confident in the power of the God who created us, even when God remains hidden in the cloud of God's mysterious, awesome and threatening holiness. This presentation, like the theology of the wisdom books, is a theology that is positive and comforting. Even in the midst of exile from the Promised Land, these theologians took delight in emphasizing that every aspect of and every thing in creation is good. As such it represents a magnificent counterweight to the anthropomorphic, fumbling God of Gen. 2 - 4 who ends up expelling man and woman from Eden and has to deal with guilty assassins.

To give the Sabbath a cosmic foundation and to conceive it as the temple that facilitates the interchange of energy between God and the creation is the highest expression of a faith that does not need divinely appointed material objects for its life, even while it recognizes that all material reality is good. Imitating the God who rested on the seventh day, human beings who were created to be God's representatives on earth enter into eternity where the transcendent and luminous God of the first day of creation dwells. The Sabbath is the Old Testament's way of presenting the incarnation. It is the culmination of all divine activities that ties it to the world of human flesh and blood.

Actually, Gen. 1 has a didactic function. Its logic is neither historical nor scientific. Its argument is the answer to the first question every theology needs to answer: How are we, all human beings, related to the world in which we live and to God? The answer is found in the two fundamental doctrines taught here: we are related to the world as God's representatives, and we are related to God by resting with God every Sabbath.

God placed God's image in space by creating human beings. In other words, God did not consecrate space geographically but existentially. God's image is present wherever human beings reveal the existence of their Creator and exercise responsible stewardship over all creatures. Rather than being under the powers of the stars, human beings are representatives of God within creation. On the one hand, human beings are one with all animals created on the sixth day. On the other hand, as the image of God, as God's representatives created in God's likeness, they have an extraordinary function within creation. They are a link that ties the Creator to the creation.

The architectonic structure of Gen. 1 establishes that God, while absent, is present in the Sabbath, the slice of time sanctified by God's rest. On the seventh day God created and rested. Is not this a contradiction? As early as the time of Jesus, Jews thought it necessary to explain how this could be. For them, of course, creation was not something that took place, let's say, four thousand years earlier. For them, if God does not create today, creation would cease to exist now. Creation is not the "cosmos," a beautiful system that functions by itself. Creation and providence are one and the same thing. Each Sabbath God creates and rests, and this happens weekly so that human beings may rest in God's creation. How can God create and observe the Sabbath rest at the same time?

This presentation of creation has its own logic. First God creates three environments or houses. Then, on the following three days, God creates the inhabitants of these houses. Finally, God creates the Sabbath to remind human beings that they are God's image within creation. Or, maybe it could be said, God creates the Sabbath to guarantee to human beings that God's creation is based on the blessing of the Sabbath. The Sabbath is the sign of the efficacy of God's creative power. This is beyond human understanding, and what faith in the Creator God affirms. God creates by God's word while resting. As the rainbow is the sign of God's covenant with Noah, and circumcision is the sign of God's covenant with Abraham, the Sabbath is the sign of God's covenant about creation with those made in God's image. This is how the human family, the world in which it lives and God are related.

Theologically speaking, creation is not an automatic mechanism with a limitless supply of energy that is ruled by eternal laws. The Old Testament does not contemplate the abstract notion of "nature," the object of persistent modern scientific investigations. Within its purview, nothing in the world gives assurance that a minute from now the universe will be functioning the way it does now. To believe in creation is not to believe that God created the universe thousands of years ago in a lost golden age. Such conception of creation is a return to the mythologies the authors of *Genesis* took pains to leave behind. To believe in creation is to believe that every instant is created by God. It is to believe that the human family and the world in which it lives is being created and preserved by God every moment. To rest on the Sabbath is to recognize the presence of God in our time and to actualize one's faith in the transcendent God who does not remain absent. Those of faith rest in full trust because God is actively creating the heavens and the earth and every Sabbath becomes incarnate with us in the holiness of God's unknowable activity.

CREATION IN THE LETTER *TO THE ROMANS*

Paul wrote *To the Romans* to defend his gospel because other Christians were rejecting it and apparently accusing Paul of having turned God's truth into a lie. These Christians, like Paul, had come from Judaism. They argued that since he was a Jew, he should be ashamed preaching a gospel which denies the history of salvation and denies that the Law of Moses reveals the justice of God. They believed that the knowledge and truth of God is concretized in the Law (2:20), and thought that it was shameful for a Jew, circumcised and instructed in the Law, to have the temerity to deny this fundamental reality. Having possession of the Law, these Christians felt qualified to judge others and teach them how God thinks and acts.

Defending himself from the verbal abuse and persecution of these Christians who pretended to maintain their privileged position before God on the basis of their being Jews who possessed the law, Paul declares, "I am not ashamed of the gospel because it is the power of God to save everyone who has faith" [in God] (1:16). With these words Paul establishes that the gospel does not consist of information but of power to save, and that this power is not in the hands of humans but of God. That is, the gospel has to do with God's actions. God's activity, however, is being questioned on account of what transpires around us. Looking around we see that the just suffer and the wicked prosper. Apparently, God is not sufficiently powerful to ensure that the right prevails in the world. Paul wrote *To the Romans* to argue that the gospel reveals the power of God to bring about the triumph of righteousness (1:17).

To place matters in their proper context, Paul says that the justice of God reveals itself in the midst of the already manifest wrath of God (1:18). Of course, both justice and wrath depend on power. The clearest demonstration of God's power is God's activity as creator. Appealing to the evidence in creation, Paul bypasses the Law. According to Paul, creation shows that which can be known of God. Paul thus tacitly admits that God is, as such, unknowable. That was already affirmed by the Jewish Wisdom tradition, and was the philosophical position of many in the first century. They argued among themselves whether this was due to the nature or will of God, or to the limitations of human knowledge. Along these lines the author of the gospel *According to John*, denying the story in Ex. 24:9-11, says, "No one has ever seen God" (Jn. 1:18). But, while God is invisible, incorruptible and immortal, "God's power and deity" (1:20) are in evidence in creation. Therefore, those who "by their wickedness suppress the truth" (1:18) can not be excused for their failure to acknowledge God (1:20).

These words of Paul have for centuries been the proof text for natural theology. When humans, rather than glorifying and giving thanks to God, become vain and let their hearts become dark pontificating nonsense, they are manifesting the wrath of God. Living in the midst of a creation that manifests the attributes of God, human beings exchange the glory of the Creator God for images of creatures. In other words, it is not necessary to have the Law, the Prophets and the Writings in order to have enough knowledge of God to cause human beings to give glory and thanks to God. The witness of creation is enough to bring about recognition of the divinity and power of God.

Pride turns human beings into fools who worship idols instead of God, and use their body in unnatural relations. By these actions they show that they are not taking God seriously. God responds to their unnatural behaviors by "giving them up" to their own devises and passions. According to Paul neither the Law nor Satan are involved in these perversions. Here the relation of the Creator with all created things is immediate, without intermediary agents (1:18-32). Those living freely in God's creation without paying attention to what nature tells them about its Creator are presented as evidence for the manifestation of the wrath of God in the world now. In other words, the wrath of God is not revealed by descriptions of God spewing fire or throwing thunderbolts. It is seen in the unseemly behavior of human beings. Creation here plays a very significant role as the witness to the Creator. It reveals the power and deity of the God who is constantly active in the lives of creatures.

In chapter 5, Paul establishes the significance of Christ, as the revelation of the justice of God, by contrasting Him with Adam. The first Adam opened the door and sin and death entered the world. Once in, they now reign. As the manifestation of the wrath of God within creation is not related to the Law or Satan, so also the manifestation of God's justice and life has nothing to do with them. Both the entrance of sin and death (manifestations of wrath) and the entrance of justice and life (manifestations of God's justice) are assigned to one individual. The first two entered through Adam, and the second two through the Second Adam (5:12, 15, 19). As of the present, Paul says, the wrath of God is being revealed by those human beings who sin and die, and the justice of God is revealed in those individuals who by faith "reign in life through the one man Jesus Christ" (5:17). Thus Paul explains how both the wrath and the justice of God are at work by the power of God in the world now. They are not abstract concepts that human beings must strive to understand but actually lived experiences.

As creatures living in the world where sin and death reign, however, humans greatly desire liberation from the slavery of corruption (8:21). All creation actually groans as a woman at the hour of giving birth desiring the deliverance of the body. Even Christians who "have received the down payment of the Spirit" also live groaning in their desire for redemption (8:23). "In hope we are saved" (8:24), affirms Paul. On account of these conditions, God's wrath and justice are not as obvious as they should be.

The contradiction in creation is that it manifests "the eternal power and deity" of God (1:20) and at the same time groans "subjected to futility" (8:20). On the one hand, God gives up those whose pride, idolatry and unnatural passions reveal God's wrath. On the other, this same God also reveals justice, power and life in the Second Adam, the Son of God in the Spirit of the resurrection (1:4 - 5), and all those who have faith in Him. We must note, however, that beside the parallelism of the two Adams, there is also a marvelous contrast between them. The relationship between the action of one and its consequences is inverted. While the disobedience of one has had awful consequences in many, the awful condition of many has been undone by the obedience of one (5:19).

Even though creation now groans desiring the liberation of the sons of God, the "eternal power" of God to save those who "see fit to acknowledge God" (1:28) makes it possible for creation to be subject under God "with hope" (8:20). In *To the Romans,* even though Adam opened the door and sin and death entered the world created by God, God is in control of the world. The creation that groans with labor pains is subject to the God who subjects it with hope. Creation has not fallen into Satan's hands.

To the Romans both at the beginning and the end exhorts Christians not to judge their fellows. As an incentive, it reminds them that they themselves will have to stand before the righteous judgment of God (2:5; 14:9 - 11) The Christian Jews who exempt themselves from judgment and judge gentiles as sinners, as well as all Christians who judge or despise their fellow Christians because they adopt a different posture about the identity of the Sabbath or the purity of meats, are exhorted by Paul not to judge or to injure each other (14:3, 15). In this context Paul, who is defending himself from those who accuse him of making a lie of the gospel and denying his Jewish heritage, makes a digression and uses emphatic language to affirm something that could provide gasoline to the fire of his opponents. He writes, "I know and am persuaded in the Lord Jesus that nothing is unclean in itself; but it is unclean for any one who thinks it unclean" (14:14).

With these words he declares that in the realm of being, that is in creation, nothing is unclean. This, Paul says, "I know." More surprising than this radical declaration negating one of the boundary markers between Jews and the rest of humanity is the basis on which Paul makes it. He knows this by his faith in Jesus Christ. His faith that the resurrection of Christ is the down payment on the New Creation gives him a new vision of reality. On this basis Paul affirms that the distinction between clean and unclean does not exist in the realm of being, even if for some it exists in the realm of knowledge. For him faith is what opens our eyes to creation and its God, and as a consequence enables us to differentiate what is the case in creation and what is understood by the mind. In this Paul shows his dependence on the Jewish Wisdom traditions which emphasize the difference between what God knows or does and what human beings may come to understand.

In chapter 1 Paul distinguishes between what is known and what is not known of God. While revealing some attributes, as said above, God remains essentially unknown. In chapter 14 he establishes that some meats may be unclean in the realm of knowledge, but that is not the case in the realm of being, in creation. The way Paul makes these fine distinctions lets us know that he assumes his readers are capable of appreciating that the realm of knowledge and the realm of being are not the same. They understand that, as said in *Ecclesiastes,* God is in heaven and God's ways are beyond human comprehension. Knowledge of the Levitical laws of purity does not give knowledge of God's ways at creation.

In chapter 8 Paul finishes his argument about the effectiveness of God's justice to save sinners by extolling the love of God. The "eternal power and deity" of God not only create; they also love.

The triumph of love, Paul says, is secure because no power in the universe is capable of overpowering the love of God. Considering the possible contenders for this battle, Paul distinguishes two groups. In the first he considers circumstances of daily life: tribulation, anguish, persecution, famine, nakedness, dangers, swords. He easily dismisses these challengers of earthly life as not real rivals of love. In the second group Paul considers challengers that come from outside the earthly realm and are beyond human control or will. Now he declares, "neither death, nor life, nor angels, nor principalities, nor potentates, not things present, nor things to come, nor height, nor depth, nor anything else in all creation, will be able to separate us from the love of God" (8:35-39).

When challenged by anguish, famine or nakedness we can do something. Before death, angels and the future we feel helpless. In the cosmology of the first century the heavenly spheres between earth and God's throne were under the control of "powers of the air", here called principalities and potentates. It is difficult to decide what Paul is referring to when he includes "height" and "depth" in the list of creatures of the universe with power to attempt to break the bonds of love that unite human beings to God. A cosmology of principalities, potentates, height, depth, etc. is difficult for those living in the twenty-first century to visualize. We can safely dismiss the cosmology, however, and understand perfectly the apostle who assures us that no power in the universe is superior to the love of God that saves every one who has faith in God, and which at the same time reveals God's justice because it accomplishes what God had in mind since the beginning: a creation in which justice was fully evident to everyone.

Therefore, when Paul tells us that Abraham, the father of those who have faith, believed "the one who gives life to the dead and names the things that are not as well as the things that are" (4:17, my translation), we can do no other than be in awe before the vacuum that separates the creation of the world of things created from that of those not created. With these words Paul presents a God who transcends creation in a most significant way. God is also the God of what is not, the uncreated, that which is pure potentiality. God is the God of what is determined by its very existence and of what is totally undetermined by its non-existence. The One who controls this frontier is the One in whom we, like Abraham, must have faith.

Christian theology of the second and third centuries, trying to defend what Christians believe as different from pagan myths, appealed to 2 Maccabees 7:28, where the mother of the seven martyrs reminds the seventh son of God's power to create that which is not (*ouk on*). From this text came the doctrine of creation *ex nihilo* (out of nothing) in contradiction to the biblical accounts. In Gen. 1 God creates using the primordial ocean, and in Gen. 2 God comes to a pre-existent desert and forms man out of its dust. Paul, on the other hand, has no need to fight against pagan myths. He emphasizes God's power to give life to the dead saying that God is not only the Creator of the things created but also has power over the things that are not (*me onta*), those things that we can not even imagine or name. The undetermined abyss between the things created and those not created is the realm of liberty. The realm of potentiality, where anything is possible and actuality is absent, is where liberty has its habitation. This is the realm of the Holy Spirit who moved over the face of the waters before creation, raised Christ from the dead, and gives life to those dead in their sins. In the things that are not is where God's power to create and to save are still one and the same, and all miracles are possible. In the totality of being and not being is where the realm of knowledge faces the mystery of God and keeps silence.

To acknowledge God as the One who names both the things that are and the things that are not is to recognize the One Being with complete freedom. It is precisely because we were created out of the freedom of not being that as creatures we received the image of God, and we have, as part of our being, freedom for not being. The letter *To the Romans* calls us to gather our senses and be grateful creatures for the gift of being and being saved in the hope of becoming Children of God (8:19) who no longer groan in the creation subject to God's wrath. Instead, we may live in, and by the power of, the Spirit that raised Christ from the dead.

No Christian doctrine of creation can overlook this wonderful insight Paul urges us to consider. Christian faith in creation is based on the creation by the Spirit of the Risen Christ as the Son of God. Creation as such may be enough to make us realize the power and deity of the Creator. The Creator of the Risen Christ, the Second Adam, is the one who Christians must recognize not only for his power and deity but also for his justice. Giving life to the dead, to sinners who groan in the futility of a world where sin and death reign, is where the justice of God the Creator is ultimately revealed.

CREATION IN THE CORINTHIAN CORRESPONDENCE

It does not take long for the reader of Paul's Corinthian correspondence to realize that the relations between the parties were stormy. Reading the extant letters one finds that there had been more than two letters and that Paul had made a trip to Corinth intending to remedy the situation, but the Corinthians closed the door in his face (2 Cor. 2:1). Finally Paul sent Titus with another brother to intercede in his favor. Titus and his companion were successful in their mission, and when Paul learned about it, full of joy, he wrote about the gospel as reconciliation (2 Cor. 5).

The charged atmosphere of the relationship is reflected in the content of the letters. In *To the Romans* Paul ties humanity to God directly, without intermediaries, even as he admits there are powers of the air who unsuccessfully attempt to separate humans from God's love. In the Corinthian letters the activities of these powers play a much more prominent role. Paul defines Satan as "the god of this world" (2 Cor. 4:4) and admits that in the heavenly spheres there are "many 'gods' and many 'lords'" (1 Cor. 8:5). Even while denying that idols have any power, and that eating food offered to them does not make one an idolater, he leaves no doubt that the power of the gods in the heavenly spheres and on earth is real. One must be on the alert not to be deceived by Satan whose ability to do so is considerable (2 Cor. 2:11); to carry out his deceptions he even makes himself appear to be "an angel of light" (2 Cor. 11:14).

In contrast to *To the Romans*, also, in these letters Paul gives these powers direct influence over the affairs of human beings. His "thorn in the flesh" (identifying it is pure speculation) is due to the torments of "an angel of Satan" (2 Cor. 12:7). Instead of blaming the Jews or the Romans for the crucifixion of Christ, Paul accuses the powers of the air. They crucified him because they did not realize who he was (1 Cor. 2:8). This gave rise to a theory of redemption popular in the first Christian centuries (but later abandoned) that the triumph of the cross had been achieved by Christ's ability to hide his true identity from the Devil.

In his correspondence with the Corinthians Paul explains that within creation there are a number of gods and lords who control the hierarchically stacked heavenly spheres. He is concerned with these enemies of Christ who still exert power over the creation. These powers must be conquered and subjected under his feet. The delay of the *Parousia* is due to the fight Christ is now waging against "every rule and every authority and power." Only when Christ achieves victory over them will he be able to deliver back to the Father a universe that is fully under his control (1 Cor. 15:24 - 26). This apocalyptic scenario is somewhat peculiar to Paul, serving to account for the time separating the Resurrection from the *Parousia* of Christ.

In *To the Romans* Paul explains that the longing for redemption from the futility of life in the world on the part of all creatures, including those who have received "the first fruits of the Spirit", is due to the God who has subjected them "in hope" (Rom. 8:23 – 25). In the Corinthian correspondence, however, other players have important roles. The world is under the power of "the god of this world" (2 Cor. 4:4), and that accounts for the way things are in this world. Even though the resurrection of Christ has established the New Creation, Christians are still eager to discard their bodies of flesh and be dressed with spiritual bodies.

By Paul's time ancient philosophers had some definite conceptions as to the organization of things in the universe. They had constructed the heuristic "chain of being." Beginning at the bottom there is non-being. Next above are found the inanimate material beings: rocks. Then are found living material beings: plants. Further up are living material beings with movement in space: animals. Higher up are living material beings with logos (thought, word, discourse, reason): humans. Even higher, but still within the realm of material beings, are found the stars, the moon, and the sun: beings which are light. On top of them are immaterial intellectual beings: numbers and ideas. Higher still are non-material living beings: the powers of the air, the angels, archangels and gods. At the top of the chain of being is God. On the basis of this vision of things, Anselm of Canterbury in the eleventh century postulated that, since God is that than which nothing greater can be conceived and since *being in reality* is greater (higher) than *being in someone's mind*, God's being is real. The understanding of reality in terms of the chain of being predominated in western civilization until scientific knowledge took its place.

In his letters to the Corinthians Paul makes reference to the chain of being. For example, he contrasts being carnal with being spiritual, specifying that bodies with different "splendors" (2 Cor. 3:11) are involved (1 Cor. 15:44). The body of the Risen Christ was not the material body of flesh in which he had been crucified. No one could have seen the signs of the nails in his spiritual, glorious body. In this context Paul not only specifies the different bodies in which things can be — he distinguishes also different kinds of flesh: that of humans, that of the animals, that of fishes and that of birds (1 Cor. 15:39).

It must be noted that the flesh, according to Paul, is not primarily, or exclusively, a reference to the material of some bodies. For him it also defines a living environment. To live in the flesh is to live in nature. The flesh is neither evil nor sinful. It is weak, and therefore easily overcome by the power of sin and death. By distinguishing animals, fish and birds as beings with different "flesh," Paul is pointing out that there are different natural states of being that stand in different relationships with non-being. This, undoubtedly, is a unique view of creation.

In 1 Corinthians 15 Paul is explaining the resurrection of the dead. He is arguing against those who affirm that they have already experienced the resurrection at the time of their baptism. Now as spiritual beings they feel free to use their bodies as they see fit (1 Cor. 5:1; 15:32 - 34). Paul is trying to make them understand that those who have been truly raised from the dead no longer have bodies of flesh. The resurrection of the dead involves the disposal of the carnal body and new life in a spiritual body. The resurrection involves an ascent up the chain of being. Even if those who are baptized participate in the death and the resurrection of Christ, and therefore in the New Creation, since they still live in the body of flesh they "groan" still within the old creation, anxious to get rid of their mortal bodies to be re-dressed with life (2 Cor. 5:1 - 5).

The creation to life in a body of flesh and the creation to life in a spiritual body are contrasted by the first Adam and the last Adam. It is to be noted that the last Adam is not the baby born in Bethlehem. He is the Risen Christ with a spiritual body. The hope of Christians is that in the same way in which, while living in the flesh, they have the image of the earthly Adam, that is the image of God given to Adam at his creation, so also when they participate in the resurrection of the dead at the final trumpet they will have the image of the celestial Adam (1 Cor. 15:49). The difference between the first and the last Adam could not be more profound because the "splendors" of the creations in which they lived are incomparable: one is in the flesh while the other is in the Spirit. Thus the possession of the image given to the earthly Adam looses its value on account of the transformation taking place in Christians. As members of the body of Christ, Christians administer the riches of the gospel, and while thus serving are being transferred from glory to glory by the Spirit of the Lord who transforms them to the image of His glory (2 Cor. 3:18). Christians who are going through the transformational process which culminates in their glorification will not have the image of God given to Adam restored in them. They are going to be invested with the more glorious image of the last Adam, the Risen Christ.

In this context Paul explains his conviction that the resurrection of Christ makes possible the establishment of the New Creation in the hearts of those who have faith. He refers to "the God who said: 'Let light shine out of darkness'" as an explicit comparison to the creation that started with the divine light that shone in the darkness of "the formless and the void" in Gen. 1. The Spirit who moved over the waters when there was no sun, no moon and no stars, that primordial light, is the source of energy that also shines on the face of the Risen Christ and makes possible for our hearts, thus illuminated, to come to know the glory of God (2 Cor. 4:6).

In *To the Romans* Paul argues that creation by itself is enough to provide every human being knowledge of "the eternal power and deity" of God (Rom. 1:20). In *2 Corinthians* he says that those having faith receive from the face of the risen Christ, who is the object of their faith, the knowledge that they do not belong to the natural world, but to the spiritual world. This revelation of the glory of the risen Christ gives them knowledge of the glory of God, a higher knowledge than that of his eternal power and divinity. This means that those who have faith in the One who raised Christ from the dead are transformed and ascend to higher levels in the chain of being, from glory to glory, from one condition of living to a higher one. This is the mysticism of Paul.

In a final, desperate attempt to defend himself from the many charges the Corinthians are making against him, Paul resorts to an enumeration of his sufferings for the sake of the gospel and to the presentation of his trip to Paradise as evidence of the authenticity of his apostleship. He does not make clear whether Paradise is in the third heaven, or in a higher one. He makes clear, however, that his trip took place while in an ecstatic condition that prevented him from being aware whether he was making the trip through the heavenly regions with his body of flesh or without it (2 Cor. 12:2 - 4).

In the Jewish mystic literature of the first to the fourth centuries there are several descriptions of trips to the higher spheres of the heavens where the travelers learn things which they cannot talk about when they return to earth. Paul's narrative of his trip through the heavenly spheres belongs to this literary genre. All these accounts are based on a cosmology and a vision of life on earth characterized by the longing to escape the earthly lower regions of the chain of being and return to the higher regions where the human soul resided before being born into this creation. Life on this earth is the result of a fall from the true human home. Here the soul finds itself on a sojourn in a foreign environment.

This vision of reality is the opposite of the one found in the Old Testament (with the exception of the book of Daniel). There it is taken for granted that the human home is on the earth. By referring to his heavenly trip and by making clear that the resurrection of the dead involves the reception of a spiritual body bearing the image of the celestial Adam, Paul abandons the view of creation found in the Old Testament and adopts the point of view prevalent in the Jewish culture of his time, which no longer considers the earth as the human home. Both of these views came into Judaism from Platonism.

In *To the Romans* Paul affirms that for him Adam is "a type of the one who was to come" (Rom. 5:14). His role was to anchor the identity of Christ as the last Adam. The disobedience of one man has been countered by the obedience "unto death" of one man. But in the same way in which the disobedience of Adam was not of the law, neither was Christ's obedience of the law. His obedience was obedience to death on the cross. In *2 Corinthians* Paul's argument is that those who die and are raised with Christ when they are baptized no longer see their fellow humans "according to the flesh" because they live "for the one who for their sake died and was raised". They participate in the New Creation (2 Cor. 5:15 - 17), even though they have not yet received their spiritual bodies as Christ received his when he was raised by God. The carnal Adam, as a type of the one who was to come, only allows us to understand more clearly "the last Adam," the celestial one, the first fruit of those who are to live in spiritual bodies

The death that concerns Paul is eschatological death, "the greatest of deaths" (2 Cor. 1:10), that is, death under the condemnation of sin. This is the death that entered the world with the sin of Adam, the death which is the last enemy to be conquered (1 Cor. 15:26), the death that separates humans from God, and from which only God can save them. Paul conceives sin and eschatological death as almost the same thing. But he considers biological death as indifferent, without significance. In Philippians 1:21 he evaluates biological death as "gain," "advantageous."

As we saw in our consideration of the creation account in Gen. 2:4b – 4:26, Adam and Eve were created mortal and needed to have access to the tree of life to keep alive. For Paul, as a type of the one who was to come, Adam plays a theological role, not a historical one. It must also be remembered that the apocalyptic notion of The Fall is not a biological or a historical one. It is a theological notion that functions in the history of salvation. The history of salvation, however, is theology, not academic history, or scientific biology. For the history of salvation biological death is immaterial, inconsequential.

In his correspondence with the Corinthians Paul concedes creation in the flesh to the powers of the air and focuses his vision on the New Creation in the Spirit, the glory of which is reflected in the hearts of those who have died and been raised with Christ. Life in the world where sin and death reign, where it maintains an intimate relationship with biological death (2 Cor. 1: 9), is not to be compared with life "in Christ," which is not under the condemnation of the law and triumphs over "the greatest of deaths", the eternal one.

In these letters Paul makes repeated reference to the mystery of the wisdom of God (1 Cor. 2:7; 4:1; 13:2; 14:2; 15:51). The mystery resides in the replacement of the creation in the flesh by the creation in the Spirit, of which the resurrection of Christ is the first fruit. His resurrection makes it possible to transfer those who have faith from one sphere of glory to higher spheres of glory in the image of Christ's glory. To remain tied to the creation in the flesh is to be ignorant of the wisdom of God. In contrast to those who lament the loss of Paradise and expect its return, Paul finds

joy living "in Christ" and expects to be re-created in the image of
the risen Christ.

Paul is an apocalyptic thinker who considers it absolutely
necessary to be saved from the world that is under the control of
sin, death and the cosmic powers, all of which are to be conquered
before the *Parousia* of the risen Christ can take place. But he does
not engage in apocalyptic descriptions of the destruction of this
creation in order to re-establish the paradisiacal Garden of Eden
with the New Jerusalem in it. His vision of the New Creation is
fully constituted by the power and the reality of the Spirit that "out
of nothing" constituted the body of the risen Christ. For him
Christ is the center and the totally of his theology. Talk about the
primordial light or Adam only serves to illumine the significance
of what the risen Christ is for the whole of humanity. It is only in
him that any talk about creation has relevance.

It would seem that to ignore Paul's vision of the New Creation
and to limit any and all discussions of creation to a fundamentalist
reading of Genesis 1 is to overlook what being a Christian is all
about. What is the Christian Gospel if not the proclamation of
faith in the power of God who raised Christ from the dead and
thus established the New Creation? Any Christian understanding
of creation that overlooks Paul's proclamation of the creation in
Christ willfully discredits itself. The past is not significant for its
own sake. It is significant only to the extent that it provides insights
with which to envision the future and live the present "with hope."

In his letter *To the Romans* Paul starts the defense of his
apostleship with an appeal to creation as a witness to the power
and deity of God which makes inexcusable the human proclivity
to worship idols. This, however, is considered by him only a
foundation for something much more significant. To have faith is
to acknowledge the power and deity of God in the resurrection of
Christ, in the creation by the Spirit of the Last Adam. He is the
first fruits of the New Creation, and it is in this creation that
Christians live by faith. It is by the Spirit that raised Christ from
the dead into a spiritual body that Christians are being now

transformed from glory to glory into the image of Christ's glory. By faith Christians do not live in the natural world of the flesh, but in the New Creation of the Spirit. If Christians are to spend much energy in defense of creation, it must be spent in the proclamation of the power of life in the Risen Christ, which makes all believers in Christ a New Creation.

CREATION IN THE LETTER *TO THE* COLOSSIANS

The letter *To the Colossians* offers arguments to prevent its readers from being led astray by those who are teaching them "philosophy and empty deceit" (2:8). These arguments are firmly based on a Christian understanding of creation that is amazingly daring and creative. It takes basic Hebraic understandings and transplants them into Hellenistic soil in order to offer a cosmos occupied by "the Plenitude" of the risen Christ who created and reconciled it. The author of the letter can only think of redemption in terms of a Christian understanding of creation.

Even if it has been quite difficult to define with precision the teachings of those who were confusing the Christians at Colossae, most scholars would agree that central to their way of looking at things was the notion that the human soul is a celestial being that belongs in the higher spheres of the chain of being. In the previous chapter we already encountered the notion that the universe is composed of levels stacked with matter at the bottom and spiritual beings at the top. Living on earth in a material body the soul is entrapped in a place where it does not belong. Its ever-present desire is to escape to the higher regions which are its home. According to those teachers the Gospel provides the means for ascending to the higher spheres from which mankind had fallen. Salvation consists in undoing The Fall by an ascent through the hierarchically stacked heavens.

The "elements of the world" played a central role in this "philosophy". Since the elements of the world are the constitutive basic blocks of reality, knowledge of the elements is the key that facilitates the ascent through the spheres. For the journey upwards the aspiring travelers must go through special training to achieve the perfection that will enable them to separate themselves from their bodies and also acquire hidden knowledge of the elements. This knowledge will give them power over these elements.

What was at stake is how to see ourselves within creation. The elements of the world are the philosophically abstracted elements which constitute the basis of all created things. The Greeks had identified four, or maybe five, elements: earth, water, air, fire, and maybe ether. Knowledge of the way in which "the principalities and powers" (2:15) of the air controlled the elements was necessary to ascend through the spheres and participate in liturgies with angels, entering into and seeing the invisible (2:18). It appears, then, that these teachers were satisfying the desire to reach the perfection required of those who wished to ascend to the heavenly regions. According to them, obeying the rules "Do not handle, Do not taste, Do not [even] touch" certain things, and voluntarily treating one's body severely (2: 22 - 23) made it possible to reach the perfection necessary to escape from the lower regions of the universe.

The author of *To the Colossians* considers these rules and practices to be "human precepts and doctrines" (2:22) "according to the elemental spirits of the universe and not according to Christ" (2:8). It appears, then, that the Colossians were being taught a mystical religion with some Christian features. The mystery religions that flourished in the Roman empire at that time took elements from ancient fertility cults and gave them a Hellenistic dress that made them more appealing to the masses who were searching for a more personal sense of security in a world where life was quite fragile on account of economic, political and social factors. It is not at all surprising to find that there were those who accommodated the Christian gospel to this general religious environment.

What is most surprising about *To the Colossians* is that neither the teachers who were confusing the Colossian Christians with their syncretistic gospel nor the author of the letter who was combating them drew their arguments from the Torah, the Scriptures considered inspired by all Christians. In this the author of *To the Colossians* takes a course quite different from the one taken by Paul. In *To the Galatians* Paul also had to deal with people who were concerned with "the elemental spirits of the universe" (Gal. 4:3). He builds his argument against them by making an extended exposition of the purpose of Torah. In *To the Colossians*, however, Torah plays no role whatsoever. Other features of the letter and this rather prominent difference argue strongly in favor of pseudonymous authorship.

In *To the Colossians* the basic text is a then well-known Christian hymn. The author assumes that the readers of the letter would agree with what the hymn proclaims. This hymn, in its original form may have been something like this:

He is the image of the invisible God,
The first born of every creature.
By him were all things created.
He is the Head of the Body.

He is the beginning,
The first born of the dead.
By him were all things reconciled.
In him the *pleroma* is pleased to dwell.
        (reconstructed from 1:15-20)

To the words of the hymn the author adds annotations that expand or explain what it says. He notes that "all the things created" include celestial and terrestrial, visible and invisible things. The thrones, dominions, principalities and powers of the air were also created by him and for him. He is before them all and the one who sustains their existence. The last line of the first stanza is explained as a reference to the church not the universe, as the hymn's context implies.

In the second stanza the hymn uses "the beginning" as an already well known theological title for Christ. The author then explains that, as a consequence of his being the first born of the dead (by his eschatological resurrection), Christ is already preeminent above all things. Finally, he asserts that the reconciliation of all things created, including the powers of the air, has been accomplished by His death on the cross. The reconciliation has its most effective, immediate consequence in the peace that obtains between Jews and Gentiles in the church, so that the obviously gentile Colossians who used to be "strangers and enemies" are now also at peace within the body of Christ.

The hymn that serves as a basic text exalts Christ as Creator and Reconciler of the universe. Its theme is cosmic. It begins by declaring Christ to be the image of the invisible God and the One who created all things A similar declaration is made in the gospel *According to John*, except that instead of referring to Christ as the image it presents him as the *Logos* (thought, word, discourse, reason). He is the agent used by God to create the world, in this way elaborating on the idea expressed in Psalm 33:6, "By the Word of the Lord the heavens were made." It may also be remembered that this gospel begins with a reference to "in the beginning".

The hymn ends by characterizing Christ as the *pleroma*, the plenitude, the fullness. Again, the gospel *According to John* refers to the risen Christ as the *pleroma* from which "we all have received, grace upon grace" (1:16). The original word, *pleroma*, expresses what the philosophers conceived as the totality of all that exists, including God. Here it is said that the *pleroma* is pleased to dwell in the risen Christ. I cannot think of a better way of saying that Christ is the Lord of the cosmos. In other words, the elements of the world should not be considered such. The author is intent on making sure that everyone understands what he is saying. Therefore, fearful that the Colossians would adopt the teachings of those who explain creation in terms of the elements of the world --thinking that by doing so they will gain access to perfection and the ability to travel in the heavenly spheres -- he elaborates: "because in Him the *pleroma* of divinity dwells bodily, and in him you have been perfected, who is the head of all principalities and powers" (2:9 - 10).

This is an extraordinary declaration. It is grounded on a Hebraic understanding of the unity of the person and understands that the universe is like an individual with a body and a soul. This way of seeing the universe, as the *pleroma*, was well known in the first century and is very well documented in the writings of Philo of Alexandria. Both of these notions allow for the understanding of the *pleroma* as a unit that includes the God of the universe. The physical reality of the universe is the body of the Divinity. Also made clear is that the principalities and powers of the air, which are integral elements of the body, are under the control of the head of the universal body, the Risen Christ. This could be taken as an ancient expression of modern panentheism. Unlike pantheism, the notion that at the core of every thing in nature there is a divine spirit or god, panentheism is the notion that God is active in and through the natural world. The natural world is the body and Christ is the soul, the head, of the universal reality.

In the view of the author of *To the Colossians* humanity is not living in a fallen creation that groans for the "redemption of the body", as Paul would say (Rom. 8:18 – 23). The death and the resurrection of Christ brought about reconciliation between God and the world, and peace reigns in the universe. God's forgiveness has been most effective, and God's love now ties everything together in a magnificent package (3:14). This obviously renders unnecessary any attempt to attain to perfection by ascetic or masochistic practices that supposedly purify the soul for a heavenly ascent. It also sees Christ as the head of the *pleroma* where peace obtains. No apocalyptic scenarios belong here.

The most surprising thing in *To the Colossians*, however, is how circumcision is used as the central metaphor in an argument for Christ's superiority, both as the redeeming agent of perfection and as a ruler over the principalities and powers of the air and their "elemental spirits." Circumcision was institutionalized as an initiation rite that integrates an individual into a community, and prior to its adoption for this purpose in Israel it had been a rite of passage to adulthood and sexual activity in many cultural settings.

In time, Jewish theologians assigned other functions to circumcision, besides initiation into the covenant community. Among them was the perfecting of the body. Female bodies were considered imperfect because they lack a penis. Taking out the foreskin was considered an improvement of the male body, a perfecting of it. That is, circumcision makes the male body perfect by adding a quality or faculty, facilitating sexual activity.

In *To the Colossians* circumcision is not primarily an initiation rite or a rite of passage, but what makes for the perfection of the body. The uncircumcised body is not perfect. Here the death and the resurrection of Christ is viewed as the circumcision of the body of the *pleroma*. As a consequence, the *pleroma,* the cosmic Christ, is perfectly satisfied. In other words, the body in which the *pleroma* is pleased to dwell was circumcised "without hands" (2:11) on the cross. The disposal of the carnal body of Christ at the cross is the disposal of the foreskin of the *pleroma*. This is a most original metaphor. At baptism Christians participate in the circumcision of Christ (2:11-15), and in this way are made perfect. Baptized Christians have disposed of their old *anthropos* and put on a new being which renews their "knowledge according to the image of their Creator" (3:9-10). Their Creator, we are told, is the image of the Invisible God. The circumcision of Christ disposes of their old being and gives them a new way of seeing (have knowledge of) all things in the *pleroma*. They do not need knowledge of the elements of the world.

Seeing creation as a body that is perfected by circumcision and seeing baptism as the circumcision that perfects Christians by the removal of their old being is a unique and amazing theological *tour de force*. After all, to do theology is to find the metaphors and the analogies that give faith a way to express itself. To open up new ways of seeing for the benefit of people who inhabit a different culture and have been shaped by a different historical past is precisely what theologians must do if the Gospel is to be effective as a liberating power. The theology of *To the Colossians* is absolutely original and daring. It takes basic Jewish concepts and uses them for a totally different purpose within a totally different context.

Something similar to what is done with circumcision is also done with the Sabbath. We note that the Sabbath is mentioned as part of a calendric string used frequently by the prophets in their efforts to exhort the people to observe the feasts. "A festival, or a new moon, or a sabbath" go together often in the prophetic literature. The intention is to recall the need to live in tune with the religious calendar.

Apparently, the Colossians observed rules having to do with foods, drinks, matters of feast days, new moons and sabbaths. Those teaching according to the elements of the world had their own rules, which the author ridicules as "Do not handle, Do not taste, Do not [even] touch" things that "perish as they are used" (2:22). His advice is that Christians should not let anyone condemn them for their observances on questions of food and sabbaths (2:16).

What is important here is the justification for this advice. Feast days, new moons and sabbaths are "a shadow of what is to come" (2:17); they do not point to something that had already come when this text was written. The Colossians are being told that the death and the resurrection of Christ is the eschatological event that has perfected the *pleroma* and provides the means for the perfection of Christians. Yet the letter also says that something very significant is ahead. The mystery that has been hidden and has now been revealed to the saints is "Christ in you, the hope of glory" (1:27). The hope of what is to come is that "when Christ who is our life appears, then you also will appear with him in glory" (3:4).

This letter argues that observances in questions of foods or Sabbaths on the part of Christians are not due to their origin in the past or the authority of the law that required them. They are due to their being "a shadow of what is to come." As in Romans the significance of Adam is to have been a type, or a figure, of the celestial Adam to come (Rom. 5:14) in *To the Colossians* the significance of the Sabbath is to be a shadow of what is to come, a shadow of the glorification of the believers when Christ appears in glory. Observances that look forward to the glorious appearance of Christ are not to be confused with observances that aim at purifying the soul for a journey through the spheres. Their description as shadows of what will take place in a near future does not have a negative tone.

The reference is not based on Plato's famous parable where reality is outside and those inside the cave live deceived, thinking they are witnesses to reality when they are only seeing shadows. Here the shadow is the anticipation of the reality that projects it; the reality is about to appear when it turns the corner. Sabbaths, new moons, feast days, rules about foods and drinks are defended as anticipations of the forthcoming appearance of Christ in glory, the *Parousia*. One might extend the metaphor by saying that once the body projecting its shadow is in full view, the shadow does not cease to be real or to enhance the reality. (For further elaboration on this point, see the chapter on *To the Colossians* in my book *A Day of Gladness, The Sabbath Among Jews and Christians in Antiquity*, University of South Carolina Press, 2003.)

In *To the Colossians* the three distinguishing markers of the frontier between Jews and Gentiles, food laws, Sabbaths, and circumcision are used positively and very creatively to explain the new situation in which human beings find themselves within creation on account of the death, resurrection and soon glorious appearing of the Christ who is the Image of the Invisible God, the First Born of creation, the Head of the Body, the Beginning, the First Born of the dead, the Body in which the *pleroma* of Divinity is pleased to dwell. These titles tie redemption and creation in an indivisible bond. Redemption is in reality the restructuring of creation as Christ's risen body is the fullness of every thing created.

In *To the Colossians* the risen Christ and creation are one cosmic reality. The *pleroma*, the fullness of reality, is the body in which the Risen Christ dwells. By his death on the cross and his resurrection, the cosmic body has been circumcised; that is, it has been perfected and unified, bringing peace and joy to the universe. *To the Colossians* presents a fully Christian understanding of creation by superimposing on it the cosmic Christ that created and reconciled it. This understanding of creation is one of the most significant theological visions ever proclaimed. Through the centuries of Christian theological development, this cosmic Christ has been a source of comfort and inspiration. Looking at creation through this lens, whatever happened "in the beginning" can be left behind. The same is true of religious performances that are connected to a dated cosmology. Religious performances have their place, but they must be seen in reference to the future created by the perfecting of the *pleroma*. The "beginning" has to do with the triumph over the "principalities and powers of the air" on the cross. When creation is conceived as the substance on which the risen Christ expresses his being, the waters of the abyss that were separated by the establishment of a firmament are no longer in the picture.

CREATION IN THE
EXHORTATION *TO THE HEBREWS*

The document we are studying does not have an epistolary introduction that identifies the author and the intended readers. It does have, however, an epistolary ending that includes the phrase "those who come from Italy send you greetings" (13:24). This has caused many to think that this document is a letter that was sent to Rome, and that Christians from Italy were sending greetings to their friends and relatives at the capital. The author, however, describes what he is writing as "a word of exhortation" (13:22), and alludes to exhortations contained in the Scriptures (12:5).

The document, in fact, consists primarily of exhortations and warnings. On the one hand it makes clear that if the addressees abandon faith and hope they will not have a second chance to repent (6:4-8), and that the punishment of the wicked will be harsh. On the other hand, those who find themselves tempted by tribulations and sufferings are promised that, if they sin, they may with confidence come near to the throne of God (4:15 – 16) certain that they have a High Priest who not only is able but also eager to make effective in them the forgiveness already obtained in the heavenly sanctuary "by the blood of the eternal covenant" (13:20).

As a brief summary, it may be said that *To the Hebrews* addresses a Christianity that is in danger of running out motivations, and be left stranded having lost even the desire to reach the intended destination. The author is exhorting these Christians against becoming discouraged or allowing distractions to attract their will and become demoralized by the sufferings of life on earth. They must keep their eyes fixed on "the pioneer and perfecter of our faith, who for the joy that was set before him endured the cross, despising the shame [of the cross], and is seated at the right hand of the throne of God" (12:2). The exhortation is "that you may not grow weary or fainthearted" (12:3). On the contrary, let us be of those who forcefully "seize the hope set before us", which we have as a "sure and steadfast anchor of the soul" (6:18 - 19). Having hope for the future we must suffer the vicissitudes of earthly life to enjoy living in the heavenly Jerusalem (12:22). Hope is the anchor of the soul, the anticipation of ultimate reality. It will keep us safe and steadfast if we don't abandon it. See to it that you don't loose faith or hope. Hope is the road (9:8; 10:20) that takes us where Christ, our High Priest, is behind the veil offering his blood for the forgiveness of sins (6:19 - 20).

Faith, on the other hand, is "the substance" (*hypostasis*) of things hoped for, the demonstration of things not seen" (11:1). This definition and its explication give us the key to understanding *To the Hebrews*. The explication affirms: "By faith we understand that the world was created by the word of God, so that what is seen was made out of things which do not appear" (11:3).

Here we learn two very important things. In the first place, that God created the world by "the word" is not something we know from reading the Hebrew Scriptures. It is not a matter of science or history. It is something we know by faith. In the second place, creation by the word did not bring into existence that which did not exist. Creation by the word made it possible to see that which previously "did not appear", but was already in existence.

This explication should cause us to pay closer attention to the definition. Faith is the *hypostasis* of the objects of our hope, the convincing demonstration (*pragmaton elegxos*) of what is not seen. These technical words let us know that we are not in the Platonic world of the chain of being seeking to escape from the material world. We are in the Stoic world that considers all reality to be material. Even God is matter.

In *To the Hebrews* we find the word *hypostasis* three times with the meaning given it by the Stoics. Stoicism had its beginnings in the third century B.C.E. as a reaction to Plato's idealism. According to Plato, the real world is the world of ideas. The material world is a shadow world. To know the material world is not real knowledge because matter is in constant flux, continuously becoming something else. To deal with the material world is not be in touch with reality but with change.

The Stoics did not concede the realm of reality to ideas. The real is material. God is also material and, therefore, real. God is present in all the material world. Therefore nature should be the object of our study rather than Platonic ideas. The ways of nature are God's ways. The best way to live is to live "according to nature". We must note, however, that their concept of nature allows for human responses to its principles, and therefore is not to be equated with our scientific understanding of nature.

The ultimate task of philosophy is to guide toward "the good life". The Stoics in particularly became best known for their concern with morality. In life one must implement the lessons found in nature. The most important of these is to remain unmoved by the accidents and eventualities that present themselves and disturb the normal course of events. The greatest of all perturbations is, of course, our death. The most important thing in life, therefore, is to learn how to die well. To die well is to die unperturbed, without fear, in complete control of oneself. The greatest virtue is courage and the meanest vice is cowardice in the face of death.

From its very beginning Christianity brought Platonic and Stoic ways of thinking into its comprehension of the Gospel. Stoic morality has been a major factor in the Christian moral horizon through the centuries. The apostle Paul appeals to a basic Stoic notion when he says that "nature teaches" that while long hair disgraces a man it is a woman's glory (1 Cor. 11:14 – 15). Paul also is concerned, while in prison waiting for a verdict on his case, that if the sentence is death he will face it bravely (Phil. 1:20) and thus bring honor to Christ.

It is not strange at all, therefore, for Christians also to rely on Platonic or Stoic cosmologies in order to flesh out the significance of the Christian gospel The author of *To the Hebrews* makes use of Stoic distinctions about matter as a basis of his exhortations.

The Stoics rejected Plato's denigration of matter; for them everything is material, but not all matter is of the same kind. Primary matter, that which is (*ousia*), is to be distinguished from differentiated matter (*hypostasis*). The latter is matter that has qualities and attributes and therefore may function in discrete ways. Both *ousia* and *hypostasis* are in the invisible, incorruptible, immovable and eternal realm. Hypostatic things are beyond sensory reach. Things in this kind of matter, even though differentiated, are not phenomenologically available to the senses of human beings. Earthly matter is not at all of the kinds just described. It is yet another kind of matter. The material world that we perceive with our senses is visible, corruptible, movable, and subject to changes

In *To the Hebrews* heavenly realities are not spiritual, immaterial, like in *To the Colossians*; they are hypostatic. On the basis of this definition, we are told that creation by the Word produced emanations of phenomenotlogical matter out of hypostatic matter. As beings dependent on our sense, the eternal hypostatic reality in which God lives is unavailable to us. Faith, however, is able to see and grasp that which "does not appear" because it is invisible, incorruptible, unmovable and eternal.

The necessity forcefully to seize the hope that faith provides is expressed somewhat cryptically. "For we become participants in Christ only if we hold firm until the end the beginning of the *hypostasis*" (3:14). In other words, we will share joy with Christ if we hold firm what faith gives us (knowledge of the Creator's realm) until the end. *Hypostasis* is more directly related to Christ in 1:3. After stating that God made the universe by His Son, the Son is described as the one who "reflects the glory of God and bears the very stamp (*xarakter* [not *eikon* = image]) of His *hypostasis*." As already said, for the Stoics God is also a material being. God is constituted of one of the four basic elements, fire. We are not surprised, therefore, to read in *To the Hebrews* that "our God is consuming fire" (12:29). Here we are told that the being of God is hypostatic, and the Son is the "stamp" (xarakter) engraved by the hypostasis of God. In other words, the Son is the track left by hypostatic matter in phenomenological matter.

It is clear, then, that in *To the Hebrews* reality is conceived in terms of parallel universes which are different. One is the immobile, eternal, material reality which is beyond our senses. The other is the phenomenological reality that suffers changes and corruption and is available to our senses. Creation brought forth the phenomenological reality, but everything in it already existed as hypostatic material reality. Faith and hope make it possible to those living in the world of the senses to seize the hypostatic world, to participate in the Sabbath rest of God, to have access to the benefits of the sacrifice that truly cleanses the conscience (9:14), which our High Priest offers "in heaven itself", in the hypostatic sanctuary that is "not of this creation" (9:11) and not made by hands (9:24).

In *To the Hebrews* the Christian's hope is "to enter into God's rest", that is, to live in unchangeable, eternal reality. This rest is one that God has been celebrating from the moment God finished the work of creation in the beginning (4:3). This rest which God enjoys in the hypostatic world has been offered to successive generations as it is said "Today" (3:13; 4:7). As a hypostatic reality God's sabbatical rest, which God celebrates eternally, is available to those who hold firm their faith and hope. Therefore, the exhortation: "Let us strive now to enter that rest" (4:11).

It is notable that in *To the Hebrews* the author envisions that the Day is "drawing near" (10:25), and thinks he is living "in these last days" (1:2). Still, he does not think that Christ has to have a final dramatic triumph over Satan. Christ died on the cross in order to "destroy the one who has the power of death, that is, the devil" (2:14). The eschatological future is established on an already existing reality, on God's sabbatical celebration (*sabatismos*). This is a hypostatic reality, and those who hold firm to the faith that opens that reality to their eyes, and the hope that gives them the energy to strive in its pursuit, will enter God's rest. But God has also sworn that those who give up their faith and hope will never enter that rest (3:18; 4:3, 5). The rest God celebrates is the foundation of faith and hope, and the Son has opened the way to it. (For more on this theme, see my book *A Day of Gladness*, University of South Carolina Press, chapter on *To the Hebrews*).

Christ's second coming (9:28), when he will be seen by those who wait for him, will be like the coming of Yahve to Mount Sinai, when the voice of God made the earth shake. Citing Haggai 2:6, the author announces: "Yet once more I will shake not only the earth but also the heaven" (12:26). This means "the removal of what is shakable, as of what has been made, in order that what cannot be shaken may remain" (12:27). Since faith already opens hypostatic reality before our eyes, the readers are exhorted: "Therefore let us be grateful for receiving a kingdom that cannot be shaken, and thus let us offer to God acceptable worship, with reverence and awe; for our God is a consuming fire" (12:28 - 29). In other words, while we must wait till the second coming for the actual removal of the phenomenological reality we now live in, we may now by faith offer worship to God in the hypostatic realm.

The parallel cosmological realities of *To the Hebrews* are also exhibited in the description of the earthly sanctuary. According to Ex. 26:30 - 37 the sanctuary consisted of one tent with two rooms: the Most Holy Place and the Holy Place. The two were separated by a veil, and the altar of incense was located in the Holy Place. Since the veil did not reach the ceiling of the tent, the aroma of the incense passed over the veil into the Most Holy Place. In Heb. 9, the sanctuary consists of two tents. The Holy Place is in the first tent. The Most Holy Place is in the second (9:2, 3, 6, 7), and the altar of incense is found in the second tent, the Most Holy Place.

This discrepancy in the descriptions of the sanctuary has puzzled many scholars and is mostly overlooked by fundamentalists. I think the explication is not difficult to understand when the cosmology of *To the Hebrews* is taken into account. Since every sanctuary is in its very essence a representation, a scale model, of the universe, the author of *To the Hebrews* could do no other than have two tents to represent the hypostatic and the phenomenological spheres. For him, cosmology was more important than historical accuracy. He takes the altar of incense out of the Holy Place and places it in the Most Holy Place for this reason. He who died "outside the gate" (13:12) and passed behind the veil by his shameful death (6:19) is now offering the blood of the eternal covenant "in heaven itself", the Most Holy Place. The Holy Place, the temple of Jerusalem, has been removed. The author interprets the fact that the earthly priests entered the Most Holy Place only once a year to mean that, as long as the phenomenological temple of Jerusalem stood, the road to the Most Holy Place, the second tent, "was not yet discovered" (9:7 - 8). In other words, the real temple already existed, but had not yet been discovered by those with the faith that makes the hypostatic reality visible. In this way, he again makes a difference between what is and what is open to human eyes to see by faith.

In the symbolic universe of *To the Hebrews* the future will not establish a new heaven and a new earth or bring about the restoration of the Garden of Eden, one of "the things made" in the creation of the movable kingdom. The future will bring the immovable kingdom that preceded the phenomenological, shakable, changeable world in which we now live. The world Christians look forward to is not a world to be made in the future. It is the world that preceded "in the beginning". The world of change in which we live now is the world that resulted from creation. The life that will participate in God's rest is the life to be lived in the hypostatic world, rather than in a future world yet to be created.

What makes *To the Hebrews* difficult to understand is that it envisions a future worth striving for with courage and confidence that is neither historical nor apocalyptic. Those who have the courage, the audacity, the self confidence of hope (3:6) can proleptically enter the unshakable kingdom already eternally in existence and find "help in time of need" (4:16). They may do so while they continue to suffer the ups and downs and the temptations of life in the kingdom that can be shaken and will be removed in order to make way for the immovable kingdom at the second appearing of Christ. On this account we can affirm that Jesus Christ, the imprint of God's hypostasis, is "the same yesterday and today and forever" (13:8).

I trust my readers have been able to follow my attempt to explain what to most of us living in the twenty-first century, undoubtedly, is unfamiliar territory, In *To the Hebrews* the creation is conceived within a very particular cosmological structure. Like the author of *To the Colossians* the author of *To the Hebrews* builds his argument on central Hebraic concepts. In this case, they are the notion that the forgiveness of sins requires the shedding of blood (9:22), something that no author of the Hebrew Scriptures says in such blunt terms, and the notion that material reality must be taken seriously. Like the author of *To the Colossians* this author also takes these basic concepts and grafts them into a specific cultural matrix. He takes the Stoic distinctions about matter and explains that creation is the transfer of hypostatic matter into a phenomenological mold. This is a very purposeful use of a contemporary cosmology at the service of the Christian faith. We may certainly learn from him about the power of faith to open up a different universe before us and the necessity of hope as the sustainer of faith. His vision of God as the Creator who invites us to enter into and enjoy the ultimate Sabbatical celebration in an unshakable kingdom is most worthy of our undivided attention. All this is true even while we consider his Stoic understanding of reality to be outdated.

CREATION IN *REVELATION*

Apocalyptic literature uses a special language and takes liberties not permitted in other literary genres. One of its characteristics is the use of mythological symbols, a feature that cinematographers do not tire of greedily exploiting. As a result, most modern readers feel at home in the fantastic apocalyptic universe. When I read other books in the New Testament and find a universe of celestial spheres hierarchically organized and governed by principalities and powers, and I see that as one ascends the chain of being one leaves behind material reality and reaches to intellectual and spiritual realities, I have no doubt these descriptions were accepted as truthful by their first readers, and that these readers felt at home in such a popular Platonic universe. Other readers took as truthful a Stoic universe where all reality is material. I have no doubt that these authors thought they were describing reality in the best possible way.

John the Theologian depended on the mythological universe of the Hebrew prophets and wise men, but he added to it elements not found in their descriptions. Something quite significant has happened to the simple and harmonious creation described by these authors. The confluence of prophetic and wisdom traditions had introduced to theological discourse a problem that needed attention. The critical stance of the wise men who investigated "everything under the sun," undoubtedly influenced by the spirit of inquiry that sparked the rise of Greek philosophy in the fifth century B.C.E., brought to the fore a problem with the prophetic understanding of history.

In the chapter on the Hebrew prophets we said they were the first to present history as the arena where God's power and justice play themselves out. In this way they became the first philosophers of history who understood that the lives of human beings are not bound to the cycles of nature, but to a time-line that stretches into the future. It was in the enthronement and the deposition of kings and in the outcome of great international battles that the justice of God was displayed. These historical events enacted the judgment of God over the affairs of humankind, demonstrating that God was in charge of what went on in God's world. As long as people could see in history the working of God's retributive justice the prophetic vision was accepted as authoritative.

By the fifth century B.C.E. individuals came to recognize and identify themselves apart from their clan. Within a personal horizon it became more difficult to demonstrate that God's retributive justice is operative. To be able to affirm that God's retributive justice works on the individual level, even though personal experience shows that on this earth the righteous suffer and the wicked prosper, the prophetic historical horizon was expanded into a cosmic one by the apocalypticists. The apocalyptic vision also fell back on the notion of a return to the beginning. Whereas in the myth of eternal return human life is controlled by the cycles of nature, in the apocalyptic scenario, rather than life being tied to the yearly natural cycle, it is bound to one big cosmic cycle that will bring about the restoration of the Garden of Eden

The most significant element introduced by apocalypticism for the understanding of creation is the notion of the Fall. In the whole of the Old Testament nowhere is the sin of Adam and Eve elaborated as the cause of a traumatic cosmic derailment of creation. The expulsion of Adam and Eve from Eden is viewed as a human tragedy, but in the Old Testament the paradigmatic sin is the rebellion of the people at the foot of Mt. Sinai, when they built for themselves the Golden Calf and worshipped it. Idolatry is the most grievous and the number one sin. It is only when we read the apostle Paul, an apocalyptic theologian, that we read about Adam as the one who sinned and opened the door for sin (as a personified cosmic force) "to enter" the world created by God. Theologically speaking the book of *Revelation* is closer to the letters of Paul than to the gospel *According to John,* or the letters of John the Elder, since in these writings the apocalyptic outlook is not predominant.

Apoclypticism represents a revival of old mythological language in order to give to history a role in the working out of God's retributive justice. Reading *Revelation* we find the heavens above, the earth beneath and the abyss under the earth, a structure similar to the one found in the prophetic and wisdom literature. We also notice, however, that the air and the sea now have special roles, and new elements are introduced into the created world. Hell and death appear as powerful places or forces within creation (1:18; 6:8). Are they cosmic places or dramatic personifications? The way in which angels descend from heaven, or from the temple in heaven, and come to earth to carry out various judgments reveals that reality is considered a unit. The universe is one. That the key of the abyss is kept in heaven (9:1) tells us that God controls everything that takes place in the three stories of his house. Besides, we read of the "foundation of the world" (13: 8; 17:8) which, without a doubt, was carried out by God. Is there any reason to doubt that the author is describing what he considers to be the cosmic reality?

Basically, this book is, as its first verse claims, the revelation (*apokalypsis*) of Jesus Christ, to whom a long list of honorific titles is assigned. Among them stand out: The Firstborn of the Dead, The One who is, was and is to come, The Alpha and the Omega, The Beginning and the End, The *Pantocrator,* The First and the Last, The One who lives and was dead, The One who has the keys of hell and death, The One who was dead and lived, The One who is seated with His Father on His throne. The accumulation of titles on the part of Egyptian pharaohs, Roman emperors and modern dictators is well documented. How are we to understand them here? It would appear that the abundance of titles reflects the proclivity for them in certain cultures. The language tells us that the intention is to identify who is in charge, has authority over what goes on and will finally enforce his will over the world.

The revelation of Jesus Christ has become possible because John the Theologian has been invited to go up to heaven (4:1) and enter the room of God's throne. From there he can see inside the Most Holy Place where the ark is kept (11:19). Apparently, after this trip to heaven, John wrote about what he had seen while in the throne room. In this the author is following a pattern well documented in apocalyptic writings. Since their claim is to reveal what is hidden, they authenticate their content by specifying how they obtained the esoteric information they are now disclosing. Their knowledge was gained either by a trip to heaven on their part (as is the case here), or from an angel who came down from heaven and talked to them (as is the case in *Daniel*). This is considered by most scholars a literary convention of apocalyptic literature.

If this is the case, how are we supposed to understand the apocalyptic descriptions of the cosmos? It would seem most reasonable to read them in the context of their genre. Apocalyptic literature is concerned to establish the ultimate triumph of good in creation, something that the author of Gen. 1:1 – 2:4a was able to do without any second thoughts. In the sixth century B.C.E. the Israelites suffered the trauma of the Exile, and in 70 C.E. both the Jews and the Christians experienced the trauma of the destruction of the temple of Jerusalem. After these events, affirming that God is good and in control of the lives of God's people on earth required a most creative sparkling of the imagination using the cultural tools at their disposal.

It appears that the abyss and hell are two designations for the same place, but we cannot be sure because we are told that Jesus Christ has the key of hell (1:18), and an angel has the key to the abyss (20:1). A star has the key to the shaft of the abyss and when the shaft is opened much smoke comes out as of a great furnace (9:1-2). Besides, there is an angel of the abyss (9: 11). Things get complicated further by the important role played by the sea and the fountains of water. There seems to be a very imaginative use of language to describe the ancient conceptions of chaos as a primordial ocean from which the forces of evil emerge and exert power over the inhabitants of the earth. Of course, with the new understanding of The Fall, the cosmos has to provide accommodations to the forces of evil which have taken on a more prominent role in the affairs of humankind. Satan and his angels now have a residence within creation.

Here is where the symbolisms of Near Eastern ancient mythologies cannot be overlooked. The primeval ocean, the sea, plays an important role in Genesis 1:1. Before God starts creating, two things were already there: the sea and the darkness. The verse ends saying that before God called light into existence, the wind (or the Spirit?) of God moved over the sea. The notion that the sea has to be subdued before God can create is basic to all ancient cosmologies. The Song of Moses, proclaiming the victory of the Red Sea over the Egyptians (Ex. 15:1-18), also has strong allusions to the mythological battle between the wind and the sea. This battle plays a prominent part in the *Enuma Elish*, the Babylonian story of creation. The sea is the source of evil powers that oppose the will of God. The wind (Spirit) of God must subjugate it, even if it does not quite achieve full control. Still, in Gen. 1 only after the wind has been active over the sea does God have the power to divide it and place some of its waters on top of the firmament (Gen. 1:6). Both in *Daniel* and in *Revelation* evil powers come out of the sea, and in *Revelation* we are assured that in the new earth there will be no sea (21:1). In other words, there will not be the potentiality for the rising of agents of evil. We are, therefore, justified in thinking that the sea, the abyss, the tunnel of the abyss, hell, etc., may not be at all brought into the picture as tangible realities within creation, but as imaginary agents that play a role in the drama that will ultimately display God's retributive justice.

In *Revelation* the cosmos is imagined and features in it are variously named not in accordance to what is real out there, but with the purpose of developing a dramatic picture of God's efforts to accomplish God's will over creation. Therefore, we should refrain from assigning cosmological or geographical accuracy to any biblical description of the cosmos used in the service of faith in the God of creation.

Another important feature of Genesis 1 is that light is not dependent on the sun, the moon or the stars. Thus, in the new earth these sources of light will be absent (21:23; 22:5). The new creation will also distinguish itself by the absence of darkness, which existed in the beginning (before creation) and in parts of every day even to this day. When God said: "Let there be light," God created a day by separating the light from the darkness, creating hours of light and hours of darkness. God called the former "day" and the latter "night." In the new earth the light that illumined the hours of light before the creation of the sun will shine constantly and the days will not have "nights" (22:5). In other words, we do not learn here about the particular features of life in the New Creation. We learn that life in God's world will be totally and directly linked to the life of God without mediating agents of any kind.

While the negative function of the sea in *Revelation* is easy to detect, the same is not the case with the fountains of water. I will only very tentatively suggest that since they are mentioned together with the sea it would appear that they also have a negative function. But the sea, the rivers and the fountains of water are also mentioned together (16:3-4). Besides, the rivers, as victims of plagues, cease to be agents of life and become agents of death. Undoubtedly creation is being used to carry out the justice of God's vengeance. The same is true of the air (7:1; 9:2; 16:17). It would appear, then, that the creation that God declared "good in every way" when God created it can be converted by the same God into an agent of death. Even the trees and the green grass receive special mention (7:1, 3; 8:7). The ultimate agent of death, the one that finally swallows hell and death, is the lake of fire. On the other hand, the "sea of glass mingled with fire" (15:2) is a place of refuge. The locations of these places are not given. Obviously, this is mythological language with theological, not cosmological significance. It serves to dramatize the ultimate triumph of God on behalf of the redeemed.

More important than all these observations is the role played by the earth in *Revelation*. Some cosmologies examined in previous chapters express the wish of the human soul to return home to heaven, to escape material reality and enjoy life in spiritual bodies or in God's sabbatical rest. *Revelation* sees this earth, once purified by fire, as the true home of human beings. The human future is not life in a spiritual body in heaven, but life as redeemed human beings on this earth. The resurrection of the dead brings out beings capable of fighting the great final battle. In this way *Revelation* gives the earth and material human bodies singular importance at the culmination of history. Salvation does not consist of escaping earthly matter, but of living permanently in it according to the original purpose of the Creator God, with significant differences from present earthly life.

The universe of the three-storied house with easy access among the levels is transformed into a universe of only one level with nothing else in existence. Even the throne of God is to be settled on this earth. With the throne on earth, there is no need for a temple (21:22). Since the temple is the umbilical cord that transfers life to those living below, in a universe of only one floor a temple is unnecessary. The earth is the future. This affirmation of John the Theologian makes him (together with the Wise of the Wisdom literature) the one who most clearly bases his theology in God the Creator, the One who can create the New Earth. Even if John's primary goal is to demonstrate that God's justice is retributive and effective, God's justice depends on God's power as the Creator capable of realizing God's ultimate aims. The manner in which God's aim is accomplished, however, reflects the cultural limitations of the author. People who while being tormented wish to die but cannot (9:5-6), and birds of the heavens invited to gorge themselves on the cadavers of the mighty (19:21) leave modern readers repelled by the sadistic overtones in which vengeance replaces justice.

Apocalypticism is characterized by a very deterministic outlook. God's designs are immutable, and God's will is invincible. On this account it affirms with certainty the ultimate triumph of Good over Evil. At the center of *Revelation* is the vision of God on the throne being worshipped by every creature in the three levels of the cosmos: "And I heard every creature in heaven and on earth and under the earth and in the sea, and all therein, saying, 'To him who sits upon the throne and the Lamb be blessing and honor and glory and might for ever and ever!'" (5:13). Here every living animal participates in singing praises to God and the Lamb. It is not for us to imagine how different animals, form mosquitoes to whales, worship their Creator. There is no doubt, however, that the creation is conceived very concretely and in truly universalistic terms. As such, every creature has a theological role to play in the drama of God's power and justice. We may joyfully join all creation worshipping the Creator who sits on the throne, convinced that all life is in God's hands and that justice will ultimately be established. At the same time we must recognize that the apocalyptic descriptions of the universe are quite artificial and circumscribed to a particular literary genre. Changing the means of locomotion from clouds to space ships, or giving the descriptions the benefit of modern technological advances, however, does not in any way improve the message of the book or make it more relevant. The theological message of the book stands on its own feet without regard to the cultural garb in which it is dressed. It can be stated quite succinctly: In spite of all appearances to the contrary, God sits on the throne of the universe and he is sure to use the power necessary to bring about justice, peace and wellbeing to every creature.

CREATION IN THE BIBLE

At the risk of being repetitive, I would like to take a quick look back over the terrain covered in the previous chapters to construct a solid foundation for our conclusions. We started our journey with the prophetic literature of the Old Testament. The prophets proclaimed to the powerful and to the people that God is a God of justice. For them history is the theater of God's justice, and God is the One guiding history toward the Day of the Lord to fulfill justice. For the prophets creation is the beginning of the historical process in which God accomplishes his purpose. Even though a powerful act "in the beginning," creation was not an accomplished fact of the past. Creation and history are joined twins. The historical covenant, made by God first with Abraham, then with the people at Sinai and later renewed as the New Covenant at the time of the exile, is guaranteed by God's covenant with creation (Jer. 31:35-36). "Creator of heaven and earth" and "Creator of the Chosen People" are the descriptors of God's action in history. God creates continuously.

This is what establishes the Only God of Israel and distinguishes God from the gods of the fertility cults popular among the Israelites. As philosophers of history, the prophets saw creation as a continuing event in history. Still, when the prophets refer to various aspects of creation, they take up the mythological figures of the surrounding nations. Leviathan, the great serpent, the deep and the abyss are taken for granted.

The authors of the Wisdom Literature did not tie creation to history because, unlike the prophets, they could not be sure that history reveals the justice of God. They gave more significance to human experience and tried to find out experimentally what was the meaning of life in time. Thus they developed an inquisitive and critical attitude. As a consequence, even as they held firm their faith in Almighty God, they thought it wise to confess ignorance about the details of creation (Eccl. 3:11; 11:5). They also rejected the apocalyptic solution to the problem of justice, which delays its fulfillment until after the Day of the Lord and considers the present to be under agents of evil. For them the present is basically good. This life is the only life human beings can count on. Death is definitive and irreversible.

Their positive, optimistic attitude toward creation and the present world makes them see even Behemoth, the monster which ancient mythologies considered one of the primordial forces of evil, as "the most excellent of the works of God" and God's pet (Job 40:15-19). Their understanding that God's power is revealed in creation rather than in history also causes them to see God as a transcendent being who has agents (wisdom, word) doing things on earth. For the wise men of Israel creation is the demonstration of God's power and transcendence. Only fools think they can understand God's ways, or explain how God does things.

In Genesis 2:4b – 4:26 we find an anthropocentric narrative about the nature and the conditions of human life. Its focus is androcentric, patriarchal, and its horizon is quite limited. God is described anthropomorphically. Many of the limitations peculiar to humans are shared by God. As could be the case with human beings, God plants a garden, shapes mud, cuts ribs, opens a thorax and closes it, and walks the garden paths in search of what is lost. At the core of the narrative is the notion that in order to keep alive, humans must eat the fruit of the tree of life and obey a command. When they disobey, the man and the woman are denied access to the tree of life and are expelled east of Eden.

There human history soon turns tragic. Pride, jealousy, and the desire to become more than what they had been created to be bring about dire consequences. In sum, this narrative represents an important step forward toward a vision of creation that is not the result of a struggle between Good and Evil or the triumph of the Creator over the forces of chaos. Here Leviathan and Behemoth are absent, and the sea, which the apocalypticists see as the source of evil, is not in the picture. Also noteworthy is that humans receive life not from the blood of a victim but from the breath of God. The narrative, however, depicts a God who repeatedly confronts unexpected situations and has to put in place "Plan B".

In contrast to the anthropomorphic God of Gen. 2, the God of Genesis 1:1 – 2:4a is a powerful, decisive and effective God. The author of this presentation rejects the gods of the fertility cults and offers a transcendent Creator who nevertheless occupies an existential place within the world. He puts aside the myths in which the forces of nature are divinized and uses the week of seven days as the structure that allows him to present the Sabbath as a temple in time. In spite of his concerted effort in the use of formulas to represent the actions of God, he does not quite accomplish his goal. We can see mythological residues surfacing in the architectonic structure sustained by his formulas. The mythological struggle to control the sea or the monsters of chaos, which are referred to by the prophets, the wise men and the psalmists, however, are conspicuously absent.

The didactic purpose of the account is amply achieved. The creation of human beings in God's image and the Sabbath as the incarnation of God in time are central doctrines in the long history of Judaism and Christianity. Besides, the devaluation of polytheism and the setting up of the Creator as the Only God of the universe is a central doctrine of Judaism and Islam. Gen. 1:1 – 2:4a, undoubtedly, has always had and will always have undisputed importance as a document of faith in the Almighty Creator and Only God of the universe.

The first author of the New Testament, Paul, has much to say about creation. In *To the Romans* he argues that creation manifests the power and the divinity of God and that this evidence is sufficient to cause humans to give glory and praise to the Creator

(Rom. 1:19-20). Its power to reveal the Creator is not annulled by the present suffering of all creation under corruption. Even though subjected to futility, it is "subjected in hope" (Rom. 8:20). This tells us that, contrary to appearances, God is in control of creation, and all of creation is good. Moreover, the resurrection of Christ gives us a new vision of reality and allows us to see that the power of the love of God is superior to all the evil powers present in the universe. God controls not only what is, but also what is not -- that is, the realm of pure potentiality, of absolute freedom where nothing is already determined (Rom. 4:17). The realm of miracles is also under the control of the Creator. No evil can come out of the emptiness of non-existence.

In his letters to the Corinthians Paul has to defend himself from those who deny his apostleship and consider his preaching contrary to the gospel. These letters, therefore, confront firmly the evil that makes inroads on earth. Due to the circumstances in which he finds himself, Paul exposes the evil powers of the gods and lords of the air. They are responsible for the crucifixion of Christ and "the thorn in the flesh" that pummels him. Considering the power of agents of evil (1 Cor. 8:5; 15:24-26) within creation, Paul contrasts the creation represented by Adam, who was created in the image of God, with the creation represented by the Risen Christ, in which all those who live in Him are being re-created in the image of His glory (2 Cor. 3:18). Given this vision of the New Creation, biological death is "gain". The true enemy which is to be conquered is "the greatest of deaths" (2 Cor. 1:10). His concern is with the triumph of God over eschatological death. In the final analysis, the creation "in the Spirit", which is taking place daily in those who have faith in the creating power of the Spirit who raised Christ from the dead, makes even more awesome the power of the Creator God. For Christians creation is the creation of a New Humanity in the spiritual universe of the Risen Christ.

The letter *To the Colossians* is notable because it uses an early Christian hymn as the text on which to base its message. The hymn envisions the universe as a person with body and soul in which the totality (*pleroma*) of divinity is pleased to dwell. Christ is the one who created everything that is, being thus the head of the body. By his death and resurrection Christ has now reconciled all the parts of the body. Having conquered the opposing powers, he has brought about peace (Col. 1:15-20). Together with the image of the universe as the *pleroma* in which peace now reigns, the author also brings out the image of circumcision as the operation that has taken away the foreskin of the universal body. By taking off his fleshly body at his resurrection Christ has taken off the foreskin of the universal body. In this way Christ "perfected" the body of the *pleroma* (Col. 2:11-15). The universe in which we live, in which there had been opposing forces, was created, reconciled and perfected by Christ and now waits to be glorified at the Second Coming (Col. 3:4). Here the New Creation in the resurrection of Christ has already overcome all evil and brought about peace. In this way the author has presented a cosmic Christ as the only means for salvation against those who teach dependence on the "elemental spirits of the cosmos".

To the Hebrews is a long exhortation to not give up on account of the troubles of daily life. The hope of the Second Coming of Christ is the anchor of the soul (Heb. 6:19). In the meantime, faith opens before our eyes the invisible, unmovable, incorruptible reality that is the substance behind the world open to our senses in which we live. Creation brought to light the world that is within reach of the senses, but this world is transitory, under constant change. What now exists as a visible, corruptible reality existed already from eternity in a hypostatic condition. That eternal reality is what faith opens to our eyes and hope is the road that leads us to it. Our God rests in that reality and wishes that we should "enter" into God's rest. This we will do when this movable world is removed and we live in the immovable, eternal world of God. In *To the Hebrews* this creation is a secondary emanation of the true material, hypostatic world into which God exhorts us to enter.

Apocalyptic literature, as is well known, gave new life to mythological language, and together with it brought to the fore the cosmic geography of the ancient myths. As a result in *Revelation* we encounter a three-storied universe over which God has total control. There are, however, several places in it which we cannot locate with certainty, such as the abyss, hell, the shaft of the abyss, the lake of fire, the sea of fire and glass, etc. Besides, the agents of evil have caused much injustice on earth, and this makes some wonder about the effectiveness of God's retributive justice. This book's message is to assure those suffering injustices that Almighty God is seated on God's throne, and one day justice will prevail. Then the crimes committed by Satan and his followers will be avenged. When this takes place the three-storied universe will become a one-story world. God, angels and all the redeemed will dwell in the Garden of Eden. History is a cycle that returns to its beginning. The New Heaven and the New Earth are envisioned with many of the features described in the accounts in Genesis.

Those who wish to present the doctrine of creation found in the Bible cannot reduce it to Gen. 1:1 – 2:4a. They must take into account the whole Bible. To take the Bible seriously does not mean to exercise authority over it and ignore the testimony of most of it so as to present one's preferences as "biblical". Such a procedure allows one to present almost anything as "biblical". To be honest about creation in the Bible we must recognize that in it the descriptions of creation, the conditions under which it took place, the structural arrangements of the universe, the presence of evil within it and the characterizations of the Creator are amazingly varied and even contradictory.

This amazing display of cultural settings used to express faith in the Creator should not be considered a liability that must be covered up. Resorting to a reductionist view of creation is not the proper response to the Bible's generosity. The variety of ways in which creation is described is another demonstration of the richness and the creativity of the Spirit that inspired the biblical authors. It should be celebrated.

In the Bible we find descriptions of creation both as the phenomenological emanation of a previously eternal material hypostatic reality and as what comes out of a primordial sea. The setting up of creation is told both as the establishment of limits to the sea and as the watering of a desert wasteland by four rivers. The conditions under which creation occurred are portrayed both as the struggle to control Leviathan and as the expression of an irrevocable will which faces no opposition. The structure of the universe is described as the chain of being that rises out of lifeless matter to the spiritual and divine realities and also as a building with three stories where, in some contexts, it is not certain the power of God reaches to the nether regions of Sheol. Creation is presented as totally good and under God's total control, but also as fallen under the power of "the god of this world." The Creator is described both as an anthropomorphic Being who experiments with the effectiveness of his options and as a transcendent, invisible Being who decrees what is to be. The effective actor in the creation is understood to have been God acting personally, but also to have been either the Word or Wisdom. The reality in which we live is described in terms of three different kinds of matter and also as a stack of spheres with principalities and powers ruling over them. The future of creation is expected to be the re-establishment of the Garden of Eden, but also its discontinuation as a sensual material reality.

The diversity of these conceptions offers the best possible evidence of the influence of the cultures in which the authors who were inspired by the Spirit gave full expression to their faith in the Creator. The ways in which New Testament authors conceive the world in Platonic, Stoic, apocalyptic or mythological terms should be cautionary to any one who wishes to absolutize a primitive conception of the world in either mythological or anti-mythological ways on the basis of stories found in *Genesis*.

To ignore the biblical evidence and to enthrone a few verses in order to give them scientific and historical value is to be blinded by agendas of power that construct ideologies. In my rapid journey over the terrain covered in these chapters my purpose has not been to fight battles, only to see what eyes can see and ears can hear. My message is: "Those with eyes to see, let them see what the Scriptures contain." It is my hope that my exposition of the biblical evidence that must be taken into account will help my readers to gain a better understanding of the Creator God of the Bible

According to Paul, to live "in the flesh" is to live in the natural world. Paul recognizes that though he would prefer not to have to live "in the flesh", he has no other option now. It is possible, however, to live not only in the flesh but also "in the Spirit." This way of understanding can be applied to our theme. We cannot avoid living "in nature," but for those who also live in the Spirit it is possible at the same time to live "in creation". To live in the flesh or in nature is not sinful. Christ also lived in the flesh and did not become a sinner on this account. But Christ lived to create the universe of the Spirit that was established at his resurrection. Thanks to that New Creation we also can be creatures of the New Creation even while still living in the flesh. To live in the universe of the New Creation and to see the world as "creation" is not the same as seeing the world as "nature." Of course, those who do not participate in the life of the Spirit can only see nature. Creation can only be seen by the eyes of faith. To close one's eyes and affirm that nature is all that exists is, as Paul would say, to live "according to the flesh," and that is certainly sinful, precisely because it is not of faith (Rom. 14:22).

It has long been recognized that Christians live "between the times", that is in an existential tension. As human beings we are certainly a whole person at all times. If Christianity is a saving power at all it has to bring about the healthy integration of the personality. It is true that religion at times causes some people to develop split personalities. Religion can make people sick, unfortunately. Normally, however, Christianity is what integrates the person in Christ and in itself. Still, part of that full life imparted by Christ is the expansion of one's vision to the realities that transcend the natural world. To live in the flesh by faith, to look at nature as creation, to affirm the glory of the New Creation is not to deny the reality of the flesh and nature, but to recognize that the present must not be seen only in terms of the past. It must be seen both in terms of the past and the future. This way of living is only possible by faith, and for the Christian the future is also God's.

In the same way in which talk about slavery in terms of economics is not the same as talk about slavery in terms of human rights, talk about nature is not the same as talk about creation. Economists discuss "the evidence" in terms of numbers, percentages and monetary values; in the same way scientists discuss nature in terms of what they admit as "evidence." But those trying to define human rights discussing what it means to "be" human beings and their responsibilities must go beyond the numbers, percentages and statistics to establish moral and spiritual realities. Those who see nature as creation must also enter the realm beyond that which can be measured, weighed and calculated scientifically.

Christians cannot talk about creation without talking about the New Creation. To talk about creation is not just talk about nature. It is talk about God, not primarily about man or the world. It is to affirm that all that exists continues to exist and moves by God's power, as Paul is quoted as saying, citing a pagan author at the Areopagus, "in God we live and move and have our being" (Acts 17:28). This affirmation of Paul's cannot be limited to creation "in the beginning." It includes the New Creation that, like the creation of our physical reality, is also continuously in progress. To affirm the New Creation, like affirming the creation of Adam, is not only to affirm that God raised Christ from the dead two thousand years ago. More significantly, it is to affirm that all those who identify themselves with and participate in the death and the resurrection of Christ by the creative power of the Spirit are a New Creation. That is, both the creation "in the beginning" and the New Creation in the Risen Christ are creations that are taking place at every moment of our lives by the creative power of God. A doctrine of creation that does not affirm this truth is not Christian.

The New Creation also has its temple, its umbilical cord, its bridge to the universe of the Spirit. As Paul says, the congregation of believers, created and maintained by the power of the Spirit, is the temple that serves as the bridge to the fountain of life (1 Cor. 3:16-17). Following in the footsteps of the author of Gen. 1, Paul understands that in the New Creation the sacred is not located geographically. Its temple in space is an existential temple. It is the community of believers where the power of the Spirit works to make effective the faith of the believers.

This basic Christian truth is also presented by the author of the gospel *According to John*. In his conversation with the Samaritan woman at the foot of Mount Gerizim, Jesus points out that the time is coming when "neither on this mountain nor in Jerusalem will you worship the Father" (4:21). With these words Jesus made a revolutionary statement. Temples are the cosmic centers where communication between the different levels of the universe, the heaven above, the earth beneath and the waters under the earth, is possible. As the scale model of the universe that makes possible the transfer of power and energy from the world of the gods above, the world of humans and the world of the gods of the underworld, temples make the transfer of energy between the three levels possible. The destruction of the temple of Jerusalem was not just a deplorable historical defeat and the loss of a building. It was the termination of a way of looking at the creations represented by the temples on Mount Gerizim and on Mount Zion. The gospel *According to John* proclaims that the risen Christ is the temple (2:21) that Christ will erect after three days. Claiming that he will build a new temple, the temple of his body, Jesus is saying that Christians live in a different universe, one based on the One who is the truth and the life (14:6).

Creationism is driven by a reactionary impulse to impose divine and scientific authority on a cultural fixture of the past while overlooking all the other culturally-structured cosmologies used by biblical authors. It is a non-Christian mythological ideology. Ideologies are subterfuges to hide illegitimate uses of power. Creationism manipulates and abuses the Bible in order to transfer its authority to its so-called defenders. Pretending to be defenders of the authority of the Bible, creationists usurp its authority for their private use and benefit. The fear that motivates them is intimately linked to the recognition that they lose their spurious authority the moment the Bible is allowed to speak for itself. The authority of the Bible, undoubtedly, is the authority of its power to convince and spark faith in its readers. It is not an authority external to its message. As such, its authority is able to stand by itself. We who study the Scriptures do not defend or preserve its authority. The most we can hope to do is to understand the biblical witness to God's power and justice faithfully.

Creationists use smoke and mirrors in their attempts to give scientific authority to Gen. 1. Such efforts reveal their lack of understanding of the Bible. In their eagerness to deny the obvious influence of the respective cultures on the biblical writers they also overlook that in the Bible creation is viewed as God's everyday activity, not a thing of the past, and that it does not have a secular view of nature. Not only that, they forget that the New Creation is the one that gives life in the Spirit to the dead. As practitioners of the sleight of hand with a confused ideology creationists are not convincing.

I trust this book has presented enough evidence to spark in my readers the desire to read the whole Bible as a witness to the Creator God who cares for all creatures and that, while taking into account the cultural limitations of its authors, through their reading they develop an even stronger faith in our Creator.

Also from Energion Publications

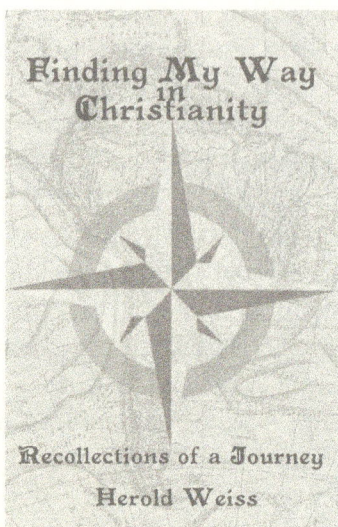

Finding My Way in Christianity

Recollections of a Journey

Herold Weiss

Reading Weiss was a prophetic touch to my own life at the moment.
— Joel Watts, *Unsettled Christianity*

From the Introduction to *Creation in Scripture*:

"I am fortunate to be writing this book as a companion volume to one by my colleague Edward W. H. Vick. In his book he takes a look at the Christian doctrine of creation within the framework of systematic theology. Thus, I can concentrate my study of creation on the evidence available in the biblical texts."

Continue your study of creation in the companion volume to this book, *Creation: The Christian Doctrine*.

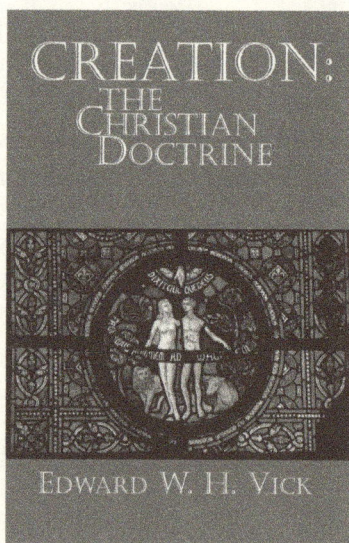

CREATION: THE CHRISTIAN DOCTRINE

EDWARD W. H. VICK

More from Energion Publications

Personal Study

Finding My Way in Christianity	Herold Weiss	$16.99
Holy Smoke! Unholy Fire	Bob McKibben	$14.99
The Jesus Paradigm	David Alan Black	$17.99
When People Speak for God	Henry Neufeld	$17.99

Christian Living

Faith in the Public Square	Robert D. Cornwall	
Grief: Finding the Candle of Light	Jody Neufeld	$8.99
I Want to Pray	Perry M. Dalton	$7.99
Soup Kitchen for the Soul	Renee Crosby	$12.99
Crossing the Street	Robert LaRochelle	$16.99

Bible Study

Learning and Living Scripture	Lentz/Neufeld	$12.99
From Inspiration to Understanding	Edward W. H. Vick	$24.99
Luke: A Participatory Study Guide	Geoffrey Lentz	$8.99
Philippians: A Participatory Study Guide	Bruce Epperly	$9.99
Ephesians: A Participatory Study Guide	Robert D. Cornwall	$9.99

Theology

The Politics of Witness	Allan R. Bevere	$9.99
Ultimate Allegiance	Robert D. Cornwall	$9.99
History and Christian Faith	Edward W. H. Vick	$9.99
The Adventists' Dilemma	Edward W. H. Vick	$14.99
The Church Under the Cross	William Powell Tuck	$11.99

Ministry

Clergy Table Talk	Kent Ira Groff	$9.99
Out of This World	Darren McClellan	$24.99

Generous Quantity Discounts Available
Dealer Inquiries Welcome
Energion Publications — P.O. Box 841
Gonzalez, FL 32560
Website: http://energionpubs.com
Phone: (850) 525-3916

www.ingramcontent.com/pod-product-compliance
Lightning Source LLC
La Vergne TN
LVHW011210080426
835508LV00007B/700